Bowhuntin' Spirits

The author hunts with tools passed down by her Northern Cheyenne ancestors. Bowhunting fed and clothed many generations of her people. Feelings unique to bowhunting still stir.

Bowhunting Preservation Alliance

Bowhuntin' Spirits

Judy Kovar
with
Patrick Durkin

Woods N' Water Press

P.O. Box 10, South New Berlin, New York 13843

DEDICATION

I dedicate this, my first book, to two special people.
First, to my husband, Herman. Without his love of archery, that first bow never would have found my eager hands.
And to my mother, Alice, who never let me forget where I came from. She made sure I forever embraced the memories of Grey Wolf, my Northern Cheyenne grandfather.
Without the influence of these two people, I would have been a far different person. They helped me realize the Spirits have indeed been kind as I travel on this never-ending circle of life.

"There is likely no author or individual to whom our Save Our Heritage program is more appropriate than Judy Kovar. As a bowhunter, Judy has gained fame as a result of both her prowess as a hunter and her gift for passing on to the next generation a love for the woods, wildlife and the freedom to pursue game. In fact, while others scramble to garner the spotlight and accumulate trophies, Judy has quietly shown how a proud Native American can enjoy bowhunting with integrity and a profound love for the origins of bowhunting. Her readers will be pleased to know that the proceeds from this book will help her to continue her important efforts to Save Our Heritage."
– Jay McAninch, President and CEO, Archery Trade Association

All images courtesy: Judy Kovar, unless noted otherwise.

Published by: Woods N' Water, Inc.
P.O. Box 10
South New Berlin, NY 13843

Printed in the United States of America
10 9 8 7 6 5 4 3 2 1

ISBN-13: 978-0-9795131-0-7
ISBN-10: 0-9795131-0-3

TABLE OF CONTENTS

FOREWORD

Way back in 1971, when the first copies of Bowhunter magazine rolled off a clattering printing press inside a Louisville, Kentucky, publishing facility, I began living a personal and professional dream. During the ensuing three-and-one-half decades, various writing/editing assignments and far-flung hunting adventures allowed me to meet a virtual Who's Who lineup of the most successful bowhunters alive during what some archery historians astutely label "The Golden Age of Modern Bowhunting." And while the hunting exploits of these exceptional men and women may seem to be familiar fare, discovery awaits those willing to dig a bit deeper. Here's proof . . .

How many noted bowhunters can you name who typically disdain the use of tree stands, yet consistently tag big-antlered Pope-and-Young record-book whitetails? How many of these same bowhunters also take the personal time each year to introduce thousands of school children to the vital role hunters play in wildlife conservation efforts?

I know of only one. That's Illinois bowhunter Judy Kovar.

Judy, who started bowhunting in 1985 at the encouragement of husband-to-be Herman Kovar, has averaged one P&Y whitetail about every second or third year since. And she's also tagged record-class black bears, caribou and mountain lions, among other big-game species. Also, for nearly two decades now, Judy trades her camouflage clothing each off-season for a fringed and beaded elk-hide dress, which she handcrafted herself and wears when visiting Midwestern grade-school classrooms.

The granddaughter of a Northern Cheyenne medicine man, Judy Kovar tells the students of the great respect Native Americans always have had for wildlife and the environment. She then segues from a history lesson into a solid pro-hunting, pro-conservation message, giving the eager youngsters a "hands-on" opportunity to touch furs, hides, bows, arrows and various primitive tools used by Americans in centuries past.

To date, her school programs have reached over 150,000 students!

I first introduced Bowhunter magazine readers to Judy in 1992. The profile I penned about this remarkable lady detailed her consistent deer-hunting successes and documented her one-woman efforts to spread a positive hunting message to youthful non-hunters. We quickly became friends, and over time I've been pleased to watch this soft-spoken huntress blossom into a self-assured seminar speaker who willingly shares expert hunting savvy with her peers. Equally impressive has been Judy's transformation from a hesitant, matter-of-fact, been-there-done-that writer into a creatively confident, entertaining and encouraging outdoor scribe.

This book you're holding, as you'll quickly discover, is unlike so many other hunting books on the market. There's obligatory how-to information, of course, but the text is much more personal, delving into the heart and soul of a successful bowhunter who has learned life's hard lessons through trial and error and benefited from her arduous journey. Judy's woods wisdom and shared insights can benefit you, too, as a deer hunter—and a human being.

Whether novice or veteran, you most likely understand that there is no magical means of guaranteeing hunting success. You must possess a modicum of hunting ability and confidence, complemented by a healthy dose of acquired knowledge attained from firsthand field experience and experts willing to share their wildlife wisdom. Fortunately for readers, Judy Kovar provides lessons that can create a rock-solid foundation upon which to build opportunities for success.

Now it's up to you. So read on. Learn. Enjoy.

— M. R. James

Bowhunter Founder/Editor Emeritus

ACKNOWLEDGEMENTS

Writing this book was difficult. The effort forced me to reflect on childhood memories and adult experiences that few people, except those closest to me, knew were part of my life. On the other hand, writing this book was also rewarding. It allowed me to relive the many thrills and challenges I've enjoyed in life and from bowhunting.

Either way, each page in this book pushed part of my life into the light, and that endeavor never became routine. Whether those many experiences were sad, happy or somewhere in between, reliving them wasn't easy. I guess I expected all those thoughts and emotions to remain hidden forever.

Some of these pages hold my tears, and you share in them. Other pages unleash the joys of a bountiful hunt, and you share those, too. And still other pages embrace my grandfather's spirit, reminding me that he is, and forever will be, walking beside me, especially when I enter the woods. Even now I can feel him coaxing me to remain vigilant, always looking for signs of my quarry.

I feel fortunate to have reached a happy trail in my life. My husband, Herman, helped get me there. We're so much alike. We started out as friends and eventually became best friends. Only later, when we knew our friendship would forever endure, did we become husband and wife. Our lives have followed many paths and crossed the intersections of several others. With luck, we'll follow and cross countless more trails.

Together we drive down never-ending roads and highways to states, cities and small towns, always striving to make our mark on this land and its people. We remind ourselves to make a difference, relying on each other to share thoughts, ideas and simple pleasures. If this book and the words within help just one person, then I have accomplished something.

I especially hope I inspire girls and women to feel the glow of bowhunting's light. They must stand tall and proud, realizing they have nothing to prove to anyone but themselves. If I help just one child pick up a bow instead of a syringe, dope or pills, I'll count that as a success. A bow provides each child a tool that's painted rich with history.

With a little luck, that child will become one with the bow, and learn well the bond we share with our brothers, the animals. Children must learn that hunting is healthy and worthy of praise. It's a natural, vital part of the human experience, and not something to be disguised or kept from view.

I'm proud of my bowhunting heritage and my Northern Cheyenne bloodline, but I also know the blood surging through my veins has nothing to do with my skin, hair, personality or loved ones. My blood is the same color as everyone's, and I share that everyday American love for hot pizza and cold Pepsi. In so many ways we're all the same. Even so, I never stop reaching out to Indian children and delivering my message: You can do anything your mind wills. Just because someone said you're going nowhere doesn't mean it will be so. Such power and determination rests solely within you. Harness that strength to improve your life. Never give up.

My wish is that everyone who tries hunting will do it for themselves, not just because someone tells them to try it. When we step into the woods, we must enjoy the habitat that surrounds us, and listen to the wind and rustling leaves. We must think about the animals we hunt and respect them. Realize the white-tailed deer is a useful and beautiful animal, just as my ancestors believed. Realize, too, that we cannot teach a wolf to hunt or a duck to swim, but we can gain strength and wisdom by watching animals and how they make quick use of their strengths and weaknesses.

Also don't forget about the anti-hunters, but don't let them linger in your thoughts. Understand that, much like the rocks, you can't reason with them. And like a storm, they will be here for a while and then be gone, only to return again to rage another day. Just be sure to give our future—the children—a chance to hold a bow, a gun and a trap. Let them decide their futures on their own. Trust that they'll have the wisdom to discover truth and follow it. Realize you can't do their thinking for them.

I try to be patient and urge patience with others. I realize my existence is a brief moment in this circle of life, and I try to make those few seconds count. I want you to know my ways and my reasoning, and understand who I am and why I exist.

I never forget that my ancestors, the Northern Cheyenne, were Plains Indians. I know a prouder People have never lived. They respected life and led a simple life themselves. They didn't want for much. They used the bow and arrow to fill their bellies and, at times, to defend their land. The bow is no doubt old, and it has been reshaped by modern man, but it still has a purpose, a reason for being.

Please realize the bow's power still comes from your body, your muscle. Do not let today's technology take that responsibility away from you. Keep yourself strong and remember the purpose of your fingers, arms, eyes, ears and legs. Don't rely on technology to make your shot. Trust and rely on your own predatory skills and instincts. Remember, you are a predator and you will die a predator. Humans are the best, most efficient predators that God ever made.

I hope you'll realize, too, that I feel a great responsibility in trying to preserve my Indian and bowhunting heritage. I am proud to stand before you and talk. I realize such opportunities are a profound privilege. Every new autograph request feels like the first. They're always special and memorable. I still feel nervous when stepping up on a stage, almost like I feel when a big white-tailed buck stands broadside within bow range. But, just as I do when bowhunting, I take a deep breath and remember how fortunate I am to be on that stage.

I hope that when you finish this book, you'll remember me and my words. I hope that, much as I still do with my grandfather, when you need me you'll ask me to talk you through the shot. Believe me, I'll ride the wind to help you unravel that blood trail!

Remember me, for I am just like you.

A few final thanks:

To Herman, I love you dearly and forever. Thank you for giving me back my self-respect and the bow.

To my "archery family," please know you have made me proud. I hope that I, in turn, will make you proud of me and of the children whose lives I've touched.

To my grandfather, wherever you might be, please watch over me and guide me on this path. I hope you're proud of me as you gaze down on this Earth. I hope to fulfill the vision you once had, that I become a strong bridge between the past and the future. I know that without you, Grandfather, they will never know either of us.

Thank you, Grandfather, for I am proud of my blood; your blood. Your spirit still flows through me. I wish we could have had more time together, for our shared path ended too quickly. But I hear your voice when I listen to the wind. When my bow arm shakes, I feel your calming hand. When I'm afraid, I feel the courage of your many coups.

And within the wisps of smoke at every campfire, I see the old ones and smell the sage. I smile at the fragrance, knowing it carries my prayers to you.

— Judy Kovar, November 2007

The author hunts with tools passed down by her Northern Cheyenne ancestors. Bowhunting fed and clothed many generations of her people. Feelings unique to bowhunting still stir inside her. They're the same feelings shared by her grandfather, Grey Wolf.

1

BEGINNINGS

As words fall like autumn leaves upon this paper, I remember many years already passed. I try to write to show myself as I am and to bring us closer. As you turn the pages, you will meet spirits that helped me write. As my grandfather, Grey Wolf, often told me, "You are a bridge between the past and the future. Without you, children will not know of us. If not for you, there would be no future, because our children would not know the animals. If that bond breaks, all will be lost. Together we survive."

With each passing generation, a new one discovers life, takes its rightful place, and then lets some of that older generation's spirit die. I've long vowed to keep those spirits a critical part of my life, and that includes bowhunting. I fear that bowhunting—long vital to my people, the Northern Cheyenne—is endangered. Bowhunting remains a tool of sustenance, and it's a tool we badly need. Our younger generations still use animals for food, but many of them have lost respect for animals while losing pride in themselves. Too often they allow a few of their peers to dictate their actions.

They must learn there is no reason to bow their heads in shame when we use tools passed down by our ancestors. Bowhunting fed and clothed many generations. Feelings unique to bowhunting still stir inside us, sometimes deeply. They're the same feelings our great-grandfathers knew well. They felt the stirrings each time they stepped into the woods and became one with all animals, not just those they hunted.

Bowhunting is a one-on-one close encounter with nature and her children. The respect I feel for myself, and all living things, comes from my life in the woods. It's vital that our elders take us to the woods as soon as we can toddle or walk behind them. The forest has everything we need to survive, and serves many purposes. It's a huge classroom and we must go there to learn. We must appreciate its beauty as well as its deadly shadows.

Mother Nature makes the forest a drugstore, ready to cure or help with many illnesses. It's also a grocery store, containing meat, vegetables, fruits and nuts. And it's a hardware store, where strips of bark become rope, or a tree trunk becomes a canoe or writing paper. The list goes on forever.

MY LIFE

I talk of spirits, bowhunting and the forest because they help define me. When I close my eyes and recall my past, I'm whisked away to those times. I smell wood burning inside the tepee and I hear Grandfather Grey Wolf's laughter. He was my mother's father, and I sit on his bearskin robe and play with the bear-claw necklace around his neck.

The author is shown here at age 3 with her grandfather's brother, Sam. Her grandfather, Grey Wolf, was a Cheyenne medicine man whose "white name" became Abe Dean after he was assigned to a reservation and registered by the Bureau of Indian Affairs.

I ask: "Grandfather, where did I come from? Please tell me of my beginning."

I was born January 30, 1952, the only child of Ervin and Alice Dean Hamilton. My white father was 40 years old and my Cheyenne mother 35 when I joined the circle of life. As my husband, Herman, would say, I was a late bloomer from the start. Difficult times and my mother's physical condition dictated that I grow up an only child. In fact, my grandfather had foretold I would be an only child, and took credit for knowing it before anyone. Then again, Grandfather knew all the vital signs—whether from the animals or the sky and stars—that gave him such knowledge. Grandfather was a tribal medicine man, and his wisdom seemed endless.

My father was a French-Canadian and his fuse was short. He had seen many of the troubles my mother endured, like moving from one reservation to another. She often had no food and few clothes, and she had to be careful to use only the bathrooms reserved for Indians. She also learned which packaged foods she could touch in a grocery store. Father knew too well that many people considered Mother's heritage to be impure, her race imperfect, even dirty.

The author's parents, Ervin and Alice Hamilton, are shown here on Nov. 14, 1936, their wedding day. They bought a 160-acre farm in Illinois. The author still lives nearby.

I guess Father didn't want his loved ones to face such cruel, demeaning conditions. About 17 years before I arrived, Father decided he would marry my mother and buy a small farm in Illinois. He figured if they moved there, no one would notice or care about her skin and hair color.

They married November 14, 1936. Father first worked for neighboring farmers

After buying their Illinois farm, the author's parents sawed down oak trees with a crosscut saw for lumber, and lived in their chicken coop until the lumber was dry enough to build their home. The coop is seen here behind a young Judy Kovar, then 2-1/2, and her dog Butch.

and orchard tenants, but he hated it. The next spring he visited a bank and bought a 160-acre farm. The deed and abstract dated to 1878, when the land had been taken from the Indians.

As I now thumb through those legal pages, I think of many people's lives, their hopes and dreams. Everyone who owned that farm before had faltered and lost it. My parents farmed and planted their new land with horse teams. They cut up trees with a two-man crosscut saw and used their horses to haul logs to a sawmill. The logs were then sawn into lumber and dried for a year, eventually used to craft a new home.

While waiting for the wood to cure, Father and Mother lived in their chicken coop. One side of the building housed the chickens, and the other side housed my parents and their few belongings. Mother said those times were difficult, but good. They were in love!

Soon after, Father was elected road commissioner and they built their home. Once their property included a few horses and cattle, they tried starting a family. Things didn't go as planned, even though the small farm community accepted my mother and father, and would surely have accepted a baby. But no baby arrived. Years passed and Father gave up, but not Mother. She remembered that her father had predicted an only child for her late in life.

The author's mother often took her into the woods near home, not only to play, but to teach her lessons about the natural world. There she learned about wildlife, roots, herbs and animal sign. These photos from 1954 show the author's mother, Alice, in front of their home, and the author at age 2-1/2.

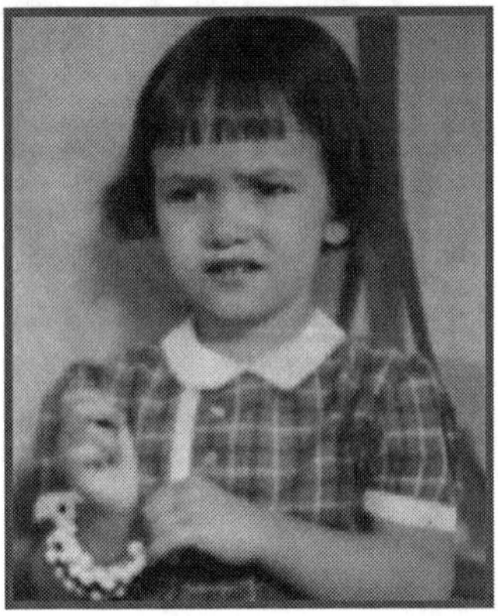

LATE ARRIVAL

Grandfather told me years later of fiery arguments between Mother and Father about this "baby thing." I was too young to understand Grandfather's message. I just knew the searing spirits eventually settled, and I was conceived and allowed entry into the circle of life.

As my arrival neared, Father began preparations for the next part of his plan. When Mother went into labor, he took a small book to the hospital and waited. After a difficult labor for Mother and some medical problems with me upon arrival, the time came to pick a name for their dark-haired baby girl. Father forbade my mother from choosing an Indian name. Instead, he handed her his small book of English names, which included the meaning of each one. Three days passed with Mother pondering names in Father's book. As she lay awake at night, she prayed for a sign. She wanted me to have an Indian name, as her father would have insisted. Her internal battle raged. Her Indian heritage cried for me and yet she told herself to hide that pain.

Eventually, the full moon peeked through the hospital drapes and it shone upon the book. The page that came to life in the bright light contained one name that touched her. The name was Judith Ann, which means "most precious." Mother thought this fit me perfectly. She could still call me Most Precious when Father was away, and Judith Ann or Judy when he was around. Mother had found her way around her husband's stubborn shame.

In the years that followed, my parents taught me their lessons with a vengeance. The simplest things for most children often seemed a matter of life and death for me. Because Mother and Father got a late start as parents, they probably raised me differently from what they would have done if they had borne children when still in their 20s. They often acted as if they were making up for lost time. They instilled every little lesson—whether it concerned wildlife, roots, herbs, animal sign or common manners—with an underlying fear. I had to retain every scrap of knowledge as if my childhood would end that day or the next.

I realize now that my childhood was short and troublesome. My father ruled with an iron will and impatient fist. Only when he left for work as the township's road commissioner did Mother and I go to the woods for lessons and play.

THE WORLD IN BETWEEN

Every so often I saw a tear fall from Grandfather's face. He seemed so troubled at times, and I would ask why he was crying. He just patted my head and talked of other things.

I could feel the tension between the Indian and white sides of my family. When I reached toddler age, Father forbade Mother from teaching me our native Cheyenne language. He worried that when I became old enough for school I might slip and speak the language. He feared my teachers and classmates would then learn I was Indian. Mother did as instructed and never taught me signs or language.

Father cautioned me often with this thought: "The more you stir a manure pile, the more it stinks." That was his way of telling me to suffer insults silently. If I had been taunted by others, he didn't want me to get mad and risk blowing the disguise he had arranged for me.

This photo shows Judy Kovar at age 6-1/2 in June 1958. The following year she contracted scarlet fever. Her mother helped nurse her back to health with small pieces of goldenseal root, which she placed against Judy's large, painful sores.

Meanwhile, Grandfather told me stories of feeling lost and not belonging in this new world where "you can't be an Indian anymore." I began to understand what he must have been feeling. I had one parent advising me to be proud of myself and who I would be someday, and one parent hating part of me and who I risked becoming.

Mother took advantage of Father's absences to teach me her ways. When we went to the woods, she reminded me where I had come from and to never forsake my Cheyenne pride. She explained how Grandfather saw things and why. Roots, plants and herbs became vital to my life. Mother explained that without them I would lose strength and knowledge. She reminded me that within our hands we hold the power of healers, which is a power without equal because its misuse ensures death.

Grey Wolf would have said the healing power was a gift, and that I was forbidden from using a gift to harm another human. My grandfather's knowledge provides guidance I still heed today, even though he left my world while I was young. Why didn't he stay on Earth just a little longer? His fate helped teach me early that life is often unfair.

I also learned early that our spirit and the will to live can be very strong. I contracted scarlet fever at age 7, and Mother thought I would die. My throat swelled shut, my fever soared, and huge blisters covered my mouth. I was too young to understand pain and patience. Mother gathered small pieces of goldenseal root and laid them against my sores. By morning the sores had almost disappeared, and I eventually regained my health.

As I lay there all those agonizing days, Mother shared with me the legends of her own childhood. Her stories helped me pass the painful hours, and helped me realize how family stories get passed down from generation to generation. Among Mother's stories was one about how she also cheated death when she was young. She was the oldest girl in a family of nine. Because the boys worked in the fields with Grandfather, my mother stayed home to mind the smaller children. In fact, because of her "sibling sitting," Mother never went any further in school than fourth grade.

With their parents working in the fields or in a restaurant kitchen, my mother and six of her siblings often jumped and played on an old spring bed. Suddenly, she bounced off the bed and through the bedroom window, suffering a deep cut on her upper right thigh. With each heartbeat, blood spurted onto the ground.

Two of the older boys ran to the field to get Grandfather. When he reached my mother he picked her up and carried her to the barn. He laid her on a hay bale and ordered one of the boys to get five pounds of sugar from the kitchen. Meanwhile, Grandfather gathered cobwebs. When the sugar arrived, he poured it into the deep cut and gently wrapped cobwebs around the wound. Within minutes the bleeding stopped and Grey Wolf carried his daughter into their home. The wound took a long time to heal, but the gaping cut left no lasting scar. One might think cobwebs would have infected such a gash, but Grandfather knew better, and his knowledge saved Mother's life.

As I grew older and went to school for a few years, Mother's teachings became more intense. Animals and trapping became part of my life. Mother taught me to study the depth of a track to gauge the animal's weight, and to recognize which paw the animal favored or used most. Foxes and coyotes favor one paw over the other, just like we favor our right or left hand for writing and other tasks. Everything has an order. Claw marks on a dead tree show not only a favorite haunt, but also a well-traveled trail.

Today, my visits to the woods take me back to childhood lessons from Mother and Grandfather. I often close my eyes, listen to the wind and hear echoes of Grey Wolf's voice and guidance. I try to notice all sign around me, for this reveals everything about an animal. I take time to look for fur or hair on a fence. Scat and droppings disclose what the animal was eating. Tracks also reveal not only the animal's presence, but sometimes its social standing. One always eats first and another always eats last. Knowledge of such order proves useful in hunting.

SILENT PRIDE

With so many lessons filling my mind, I struggled to remain silent at the supper table each evening. I had learned so much and was so proud of my accomplishments. But I had to keep quiet. Father would not understand Mother's teachings, and I didn't want to get her into trouble.

Why couldn't Father be proud of me and my heritage? My heart bloomed with pride, yet my tongue laid still. I heard Grandfather's words: "The fight within you will be long and rough. Remember from where you have come, and the old ones before you and their battles." ■

2

CHILDHOOD LESSONS, LIFETIME MEMORIES

Because Father was working all the time, toys and playtime for me weren't high on his priority list. Still, I continually asked for a swing in the old maple tree in our front yard, until Mother told me I didn't need one . . . that there were all kinds of swings in the forest.

The next weekend we were in the woods, cutting trees for firewood and cookstove kindling. As my parents stacked wood on the trailer, I walked around whining about the swing I didn't have at home, and asking where were I could find the woods' many swings. Mother took my gloved hand, walked me to a towering white oak, and showed me a large wild-grape vine. The vine twisted high into the branches of the massive tree.

Alice Dean Hamilton encouraged her daughter to have fun in nature's playground. But whether Judy swung on grapevines or a chain swing in her yard, she sometimes needed to be rescued by her mother.

Mother then took the double-bit ax, cut the vine loose from its roots in the ground, and handed the loose end to me. I grabbed it and swung, and couldn't believe the great feeling! The mighty eagle had nothing over me as I experienced that free-flying, soaring sensation. Or was it more akin to the guy in those Tarzan movies?

"Now run fast and swing over that ravine," Mother told me. The ravine was deep but the walls were tight and the ground below was coated with last fall's leaves. While my parents finished cutting and stacking wood, I kept playing on the grape vine until I needed a new challenge. I then started grabbing different vines that were hanging loose and gave them a test swing. After one big vine caught my eye, I asked Mother to cut it loose. I then proceeded to figure out how to swing over a brush pile and the ravine behind it, and then land

Teacher Judy: The author has spent much of her adult life visiting schools to teach children about her Cheyenne heritage and to share stories from her own childhood. Those stories are as rich in humor as they are in valuable lessons learned through firsthand experience.

on the opposite ridgeline. That was the plan, and it sounded good to me.

I yelled at Mother to watch as I grabbed the vine and ran as fast as my legs could churn. And because I was playing the great Tarzan, I gave his yell too. I had almost made it across the ravine when the vine snapped, and I plunged into the large brush pile that my parents had built at the bottom. Mother ran over to the ravine's edge to find me, but I had disappeared! Finally she saw one arm and then a leg emerge, and then I crawled out of the brush pile, still intact. She started laughing and asked how Tarzan felt now.

"See, I told you Indians are not made to fly. Now maybe you'll believe me," she said. "The great eagle laughs at you too. Only he knows the wind, and only he owns the sky, but it's good that you know now what the eagle feels."

To this day I have never swung on another grape vine.

But one day I did receive my coveted front-yard swing in the maple tree. I must have been about age 10 by then. Father found some used chain to build one and hung the swing between the tree and a woven-wire fence. If I swung low and slow I was fine, but I pushed hard one day and flew over the fence and over the gravel road. I should have jumped off and taken my chances, but I was afraid. Instead, I hung on and hit the fence backward.

The swing dumped its load, and the fence caught my foot as I fell. There I hung upside down, yelling at the top of my lungs for Mother. Extracting my foot wasn't easy. She had to find a pliers and wire-cutting tool to get me out.

I'm sure those early run-ins with swings were warnings that I wasn't meant to fly. I eventually learned to leave the skies to eagles.

SLEDS AND BICYCLES

Along the way I also learned the hazards of ground-based speed. Whenever snow covered the ground, I asked about getting a sled. We never had money for one, but still I asked.

"You don't need a fancy sled," Mother finally said. "Go to the barn and bring me the corn-scoop shovel."

I retrieved the shovel and Mother took me to the hill overlooking a dam with a small pond behind it.

"Now, Judy, put the shovel down with the handle in front of you, and get in," she said.

This wasn't easy, even for a skinny child, but I did it. Mother got behind me and pushed me down the hill at a fast clip. "Hey! This might work," I thought. But just about then I hit a frozen bump and the shovel's oak handle slammed me between the eyes. Even with stars and pink elephants whirling about my head, I saw the dam's woven-wire fence approaching fast!

As I rode my shovel-sled headlong into the fence, the oak handle again slammed me between the eyes and bloodied my nose as well. I sat there, stunned by the blows, not realizing my feet and legs were now sticking through the fence. I couldn't move! Once Mother realized I had survived, she again found the humor in my predicament and couldn't stop laughing. Finally, I extracted my legs, got up, wiped the blood from my nose and threw the shovel into the icy pond. Of course, when spring arrived I had to wade into the pond and retrieve it.

Later, when I was about 12, my parents gave me a bicycle for my birthday. Father helped me get on and then pushed me along. I assumed he was running alongside, but I panicked when I turned around and saw he wasn't there. I turned into the corner of our yard and plunged into Mother's prize rose bush. I picked thorns out of my hide for weeks.

WHEN NOT TO FIT IN

Not all of my mishaps could be blamed on speed and flying. My own mother and her sister, Aunt Betty, decided one time that if they gave their kids home perms, we would look more like other children. I felt tortured. The rollers hurt and the odors of that curling lotion were enough to kill anyone. Still, we endured.

While waiting for the lotion to set, I went outside to play on the old cedar tree. I became hot and sweaty, and then went back inside when it was time to remove the rollers. As Aunt Betty removed them, I was horror-stricken. My hair was burned orange and was now a mass of frizzy globs. My Aunt blamed it on me for overheating while playing outside.

Mother took me home, and when Father saw me all heck broke loose. Mother started cutting my hair, trying to rid my little head of the huge ball of orange frizz. Needless to say, that was the last perm Mother and Aunt Betty gave me. I remember telling her, "If being like other children requires torture, I don't ever want to be like them!"

ADVENTURES WITH LIVESTOCK

Livestock, fowl and animals were a big part of our daily lives on the farm. Grandfather always had to have a goose for Christmas, but this wasn't a case of picking one up in frozen goods at the supermarket. No, we had to earn ours, and geese aren't always meek and easygoing. They like to bite legs and feet, which is one heck of a pinch! That was just their nature.

Therefore, Grandfather's desire for a Christmas goose meant year-round work and goose hassles for his grandkids. We had to take them to the river each morning, retrieve them each evening, and put them into the chicken house overnight for safekeeping.

One evening everyone was gone except Grandfather, so he had to retrieve the geese and ducks. He had problems getting them into the chicken house, and so a job his grandkids did in minutes turned into a multi-hour ordeal for him. He was so angry that he grabbed a small shoe-cobbler hammer and whacked one webbed foot of every duck and goose on the farm. He reasoned that if their feet were sore, they wouldn't run off to the river anymore. We were all upset with him. Obviously, it was fine for us to have to run those birds day and night, but when he had to do it just once, the birds paid dearly for his frustration.

The author has learned how to make animals and wildlife less scary for children who have never before been near animals, pelts and furs. Neither have most of them ridden horses or tried to round up stray livestock. Judy Kovar tells them of her many run-ins with horses and cows when she was growing up.

We also raised turkeys, and Mother's pride was a large gobbler she had hand-raised. This gobbler was stupid, however. It was content to just strut all day, and never mated with the hen turkey. One evening he was "bugging" in the backyard and Mother noticed what she thought were lice on its legs. She immediately wanted to doctor him, which worried me a bit. I was about 13 then, and knew Mother's doctoring was hit and miss. She retrieved a small bottle of Black Leaf 40 from the house.

We had used it before to spray the chicken house's roosts for mites and lice, so Mother decided we would paint Black Leaf 40 on the gobbler's legs at full strength. I questioned her regarding the dosage and application method, and was rewarded with "the stare." Her eyes bored into me, her brows arched, and her lips formed a thin, tight line canting to one side. I knew that if she raised an arm and rested a hand on her hip, watch out!

The gobbler must have had some vague awareness that this would not be his night, and tried to elude my grasp. I finally caught him, and neither of us was happy about it. I held that big bird as my mother painted his legs and feet. When Mother finished, she instructed me to put him down. I bent over and set him on the grass. The gobbler fanned out, turned around to my mother and fell over dead! And I mean dead. That bird was stone cold, glazed-eye, no-coming-back deceased!

Mother looked at me, then to the gobbler and then back to me. "Well, Honey, do you think we doctored him enough?" she asked. "Maybe we should go into business."

We cleaned and picked that bird before bedtime.

BIGGER TROUBLES

On another occasion, I got something I had always longed for: a horse.

When some money became available, Father bought me a small horse that wasn't yet broken for riding. I was 14 and didn't care. I thought it was great. This little beast was named Blaze because of a white marking down his forehead.

Blaze knew my father was boss, and behaved beautifully when he was near. But when I was alone with him, Blaze bit, kicked and generally made me miserable. Father told me animals sense fear, and that I must show him who was boss.

One day I saddled my horse and climbed on, but forgot to close the orchard gate. Blaze saw his chance and raced for the opening, with me not quite ready for the ride!

Father yelled at me to pull back on the reins and seesaw them. Unfortunately, by this time I was nearly flat on my back atop the horse, seeing only blue sky above.

Blaze raced toward the orchard, me still hanging on despite moving at the speed of light. As he streaked through the apple, apricot and cherry trees, he tried to scrape me off by running under branches and through every tight spot he could find. But Father wasn't far behind.

When Blaze finally realized Father was near, he stopped his antics and walked over to the boss. As soon as he stopped, I slid off his back even though Father encouraged me to stay on and ride him back to the barn. No way! Blaze and I divorced that day. Father said I was too afraid of Blaze and the horse would always know it, so he traded him for a calf. Father saw no sense in caring for something that had no use. On a real farm, everything must earn its keep or risk the ax or permanent replacement.

On another occasion, some calves got out and made it clear they had no intention of returning. They were living in the woods and Father said it might be necessary to shoot them. "Wild" cows simply can not be tolerated by their owners or the neighbors. Around midnight one night, I was awakened by mooing. The wayward calves were in my garden, eating my sweet corn. I dressed and sneaked outside, rope in hand.

I slipped down the adjoining row and lassoed the first bull-calf I encountered. He weighed about 500 pounds and took off with me in tow. As we passed a small tree in the backyard, I quickly wrapped my rope around it, my hands bleeding from rope cuts and burns. The calf leaped at me and wound the rope around my feet. Down I went and in he came, trampling me for what seemed an hour. Finally, I grabbed for the noose around his throat and swung all my weight onto it. The calf coughed and choked as I cut off his oxygen. As he weakened, I got up and finished tying him to the tree.

The ruckus awakened my parents, who soon realized I needed to see a doctor. We learned my chest muscles had separated from my ribs, but no bones were broken.

The next few weeks were painful, reminding me to never again lasso a calf that's bigger than me. As I endured the pain, I wished Grandfather were still alive. Given how much trouble I had with one 500-pound bull-calf, I wondered how he and my ancestors dealt with buffalo or wild mustangs.

FAITHFUL, FATEFUL DOGS

Although my parents weren't quick to buy swings or sleds, they always made sure I had a dog. Mother would say, "Every child should have a dog, for with the dog comes ripped blue jeans and runners in socks. It's part of growing up. It's in the circle!"

One such dog, a rusty-colored mix between a raccoon dog and a cocker spaniel, was named Rusty. He was my best friend, and Father admired his courage in fighting groundhogs or chasing our old sow back into the pen. Unfortunately, all of that changed one day while I was doing chores in the chicken house.

As always, a few hens hadn't gone to the chicken house to use its ample supply of nests. Instead, they laid their eggs in the barn or the brooder house. So after gathering eggs from the chicken house, I headed to the brooder house.

When I opened the door a bit to look in, Rusty jumped at me from inside, hitting the screen and closing the door. He was acting very angry and I saw he was foaming at the mouth. I dropped the egg bucket and ran to the house to get Mother. She went to the screen door and Rusty jumped and snarled at her, too.

She now understood the situation. A few weeks earlier, Rusty had helped kill a skunk that had gotten into our chicken house. Mother said the skunk must have been sick, and then spoke the dreaded words: rabies. We made sure Rusty could not get out of the brooder house and then waited for Father to come home from working on the road grader. When he arrived, I was told to go into the kitchen while Mother told him the sad news. Father went to the bedroom and took down the .22-caliber rifle from the gun rack.

The author's parents weren't quick to buy her swings or sleds, but they made sure she had a dog to call her own. Her mother believed dogs must be part of every child's life. Judy is shown here with her friend, Rusty.

I begged Father not to shoot Rusty, clinging to his pants pocket, tears flowing down my cheeks. Father said, "It has to be done." Again, I was told to stay in the kitchen as he opened the back door and went outside. Only seconds passed and then I heard the rifle's popping noise. I cried harder, not understanding why this was happening.

Father soon called to me and Mother, and told us to get brush, wood and oil so we could burn Rusty's body. I saw tears falling from his face, too. He had hated to shoot Rusty. Father said Rusty was one of the best dogs we ever owned, and it would be hard to replace him. I'll never forget that day or the crazy look in good ol' Rusty's eyes.

Judy's dog Rusty was faithful and protective. Unfortunately, his tangle with a skunk one day left him rabid. As Judy learned, pets make great friends, but they also bring heartache, which is part of the circle of life.

Another great dog in our home was named Shep, and he met an untimely death, too. Father, you see, used fire to flush groundhogs from their holes instead of digging them out. He poured gasoline and water into the hole and then struck a match. On this occasion, Shep and two other dogs had been fighting this groundhog when it finally ducked into a hole to seek refuge in its den. Father poured his concoction down the hole and set it ablaze. Within a few minutes, the flaming groundhog rushed out and ran into a big brush pile. The dogs followed him into the brush pile, which then burst into flames.

Shep and the other two dogs died in that fire, reducing Father to tears. He never again burned out a groundhog.

FLYING HAZARDS

We also encountered some true scares in my beloved woods. In spring and summer, Mother and I always dug roots there, and by the time I was a teenager I hated this chore.

One day we went deep into the woods to hunt for ginseng and goldenseal for our various teas and home medicines. We had dug roots most of the morning and were ready to head home when Mother saw an older stalk of goldenseal about midway up the ridge. I was about five to six feet from her when she took the digger and drove it into the sun-baked earth. When she brought the digger up to extract the root, all I saw was a ball of wasps! It being a dry summer, yellow jackets had built a nest around the root for moisture. The angry, aggressive wasps instantly filled the air. Mother yelled for me to run, knowing I react to bee stings and the wrong one could be fatal. She dropped the digger and ran, too, but I could see her back was covered by the stinging yellow jackets.

I was crying when she was forced to yell to me for help. As I approached, I saw at least 50 to 75 yellow jackets on her back and legs. She told me to brush them off with a stick. That was her only hope. Mother's face was swelling fast and I feared the worst, but she took some ginseng roots from her sack and mashed them on some rocks to make a paste. She mixed it with water from our canteen and added dirt to make a thick poultice, then directed me to smear the poultice on her stings.

I thought Mother was going to die, but she never got sick. She itched for a few days, but apparently never suffered from the stings. I've never forgotten the lessons from that day. When I dig roots today, I always stand and watch the plant for holes or bees buzzing about.

I still hunt for roots and herbs, and keep a small supply of goldenseal root to treat canker sores. I also dry and crush the leaves, and store them for tea to treat upset stomachs. I look at all the bloodroot in our area and laugh. Why? If everyone knew bloodroot is the key ingredient in tartar-control toothpastes, they could treat the problem themselves. Ginseng, of course, remains an all-around medicinal root still in demand worldwide. When taken often over a long period of time, it also eases migraine headaches and lowers blood pressure.

When visiting the woods to scout for deer or analyze sign they leave, the author also looks for roots and plants for foods and medicines. The more one knows about the woods' plants, the more one understands the animals and their surroundings.

What other lifesavers grow in the woods? If you have an "emergency" while bowhunting and forget to bring toilet paper, look for mullion leaves, the softest toilet-paper substitute Mother Earth can supply. Boiled mullion leaves can also be used to relieve boils and abscesses.

A springtime ritual for Mother and me was to dig for roots before sassafras leaves started to bud. We dug up the sassafras roots and made spring tonic from them. If I was allowed to add plenty of sugar, it didn't taste too bad, but without sugar it tasted like medicine. We also used blackberry leaves and lemon grass for teas and ailments.

In fact, the list of beneficial plants found in the deer woods seems endless. Many of the old recipes are coming back today as science realizes the importance of herbal medicines. I've also noticed more herbal teas in bigger grocery stores. Maybe these roots and herbs are like the Old Ones, my ancestors. They might leave for a while, but they will be back.

You can never get rid of us! ■

3

SCHOOL DAYS AND LIFE'S MARCH

I attended two schools during my childhood. In one of them I discovered the importance of books, where—much like other children—I learned reading, writing and arithmetic.

The other school taught me the importance of Mother Earth, where I learned the secrets of wind, rain, rocks, twigs, leaves and animals. The whole outdoors was my textbook. I learned to put myself in the animals' place, their habitat. By learning about its surroundings through hands-on experience and observation, I better understood each animal.

I also quickly realized the outdoors provided a friendlier learning environment. Schoolyards, classrooms—or even our own homes—can be cruel and intimidating. My mother thought she could always protect me from such pain, but she was wrong. Even in first grade the other children noticed I was different from them. Mother regularly cut my straight black hair and helped keep it neat, but no matter what she tried, I wasn't like other girls. My clothes were a dead giveaway. I didn't wear buckskins, but neither did I wear lace-covered dresses. Mother usually dressed me in blue jeans and flannel shirts.

This fading photo shows the author at age 5 in 1957, holding her first bow. Her mother made the headdress out of chicken feathers. The photo is also remarkable in that Judy was wearing a dress. Her mother usually had her wearing blue jeans and flannel shirts.

But jeans and flannel weren't the extent of my differences. Just as Grey Wolf and my mother had been judged for their clothes and skin color, so was I judged for mine. Children can be ruthless.

When my mind drifts back to that time, I picture myself sitting and listening to my grandfather's comforting words as he told me about a dream—his vision about me. Grandfather said I must be strong. He told me to live for the days when I would become a warrior.

A female warrior? No way! I didn't believe it. Such things were almost unheard of. Again, though, Grandfather patted me on the head and told of things to come.

Grey Wolf wasn't the only adult who helped me cope. My second-grade teacher, Mrs. Tekla Ballard, often took me aside to tell me I was special. She predicted great things would come my way, and said my clothes and skin color had nothing to do with my inner self. She was often amazed by my perceptions, especially the way I saw animals and plants, and learned from stories. She said children made fun of me because they didn't understand me. When people don't understand, ignorance opens their mouths, not their minds.

Her mother kept young Judy's straight black hair cut short and neat, but she still never looked like other girls in her class. She seldom wore dresses with lace and other feminine flairs. Even when she did, the other children noticed her skin color and dark black hair. This photo was taken in May 1955.

BATTLING BACK

Mrs. Ballard made life a bit easier, but like all good things, second grade didn't last forever. My third- and fourth-grade classmates continued to make mean comments and I began to fight back, forcing my parents to continually visit Kmart.

Why? Well, I carried a satchel for my books, and about the second time someone called me a half-breed or prairie nigger, or spit or threw rocks at me, I thumped the offender with my satchel, almost always breaking its plastic handle. Mother said she could always tell if I had a good day at school by looking at my satchel. Many other times I just raced through the school's double-glass doors at the end of the day and ran toward Mother and our car.

As the years went by, I hid my real self while trying to be like other children. When things got so bad I thought I couldn't take it, I headed to the woods, where I always felt safe.

Even better, birds and animals never made fun of me. I often sat on a log and thought about my early childhood and the short time I had with Grandfather. I recalled his stories and the legends of our tribe. As I sat there, I watched a hen turkey and listened to her talking to her brood with feeding calls and danger clucks. I watched squirrels gathering winter foods. I saw raccoons playing, and listened to their language.

I especially loved seeing white-tailed deer, an astonishing animal that deserves utmost respect. One whitetail, by itself, can feed the hungry and clothe the forsaken. And much like the buffalo, the whitetail provides materials for just about everything imaginable. For example, our predecessors used its bones to make scrapers and needles, and its antlers and shoulder blades as gardening tools.

As I sat and thought, I began to better understand what Mother and Grandfather had been teaching me. When I was alone in the woods, I was one-on-one with the animals

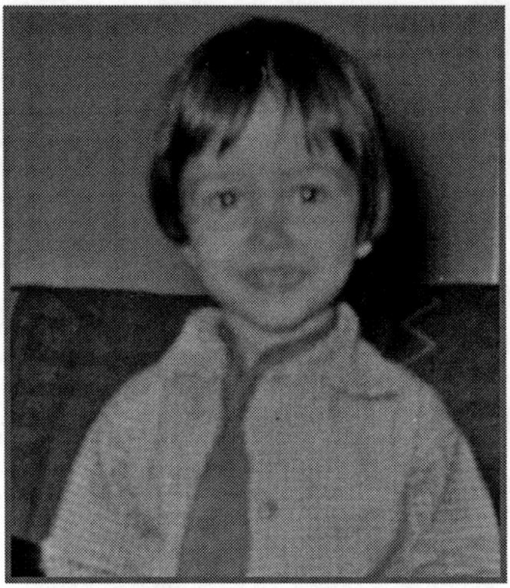
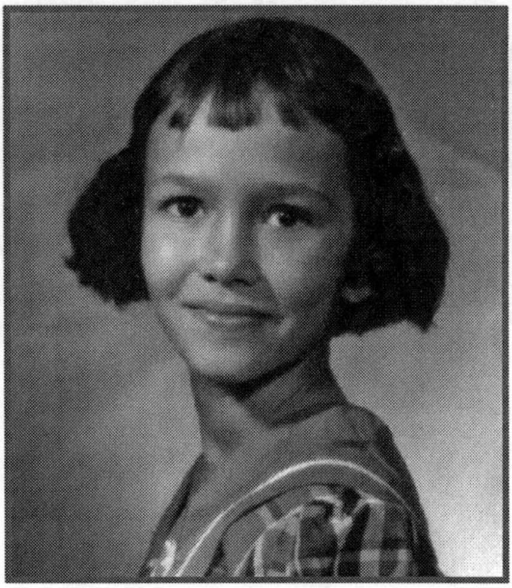

One reason the author enjoyed spending time in the woods as a child was that it spared her the pain of schoolyard taunts. This pretty little girl is smiling in these photos, but she recalls much emotional pain at home and at school. From left, Judy is shown at age 3 in 1955 and age 8 in 1960.

in their habitat. I became one of Mother Nature's children, a pupil in her classroom. Mother Nature saw no skin colors or lines of defense. I was a girl. Nothing more, nothing less. When I was in the outdoors, I had nothing to prove to anyone.

Unfortunately, my world couldn't stay within that sanctuary. I still had to go to school and I had to be among other kids. As I grew older I sometimes resented my heritage. My mother's race always seemed to bring big problems. Being an Indian meant being inferior. I tried to be like other kids in dress and in actions, but my insides always ate away at me. I tried drinking and smoking, but that only brought sickness. Somehow I knew making myself ill inside and out was foolish. If belonging among the whites required drinking, they could leave me out.

SILENT PLEAS

I also learned not to complain to my parents about school and cruel classmates because it sent Father into a rage. He thought I brought grief to myself. Little did he know the seeds he planted years before were causing my internal fights. All my life he tried shaming away my Indian heritage. "That's a strike against you, and you're a woman, too," he would say. "No one wants to see you, let alone hear you. All you have to look forward to is graduating high school and getting married."

When I was alone, I silently asked for help: "Spirits, help me! Grandfather, help me! Where do I belong and what is my purpose here on Earth? Life must offer more than this!"

Father also controlled most of my social life. I was not allowed to attend prom until I was a high-school senior. Whenever a boy wanted to ask me out, he had to ask Dad first. Most never made it past him. He had a way of scaring them off.

My short, dark-skinned father would stand in the doorway to meet them,

When the author was a teenager and boys wanted to ask her on a date, they first had to talk to her strict father, Ervin. Most didn't make it past him, and even fewer asked for a second date. These photos, from left, were taken when Judy was 14, in 1966, and, right at 17, in 1969.

always with something in his hand. His usual greeting to boys went something like this: "Yeah, what the hell do you want, and who told you to come up here in the first place?"

Some boys cleared that first hurdle, but then came the next test: Father's "sit-down-we-need-to-talk-about-a-few-things-before-you-take-Judy-out" lecture. This talk included what he expected from the young man, what time we were expected back, and what the punishment would be if the boy didn't get me back in time.

Father accepted no excuses, and he never kidded. One night my date and I were late because of a flat tire. Before we made it home, Dad was on the road hunting for the no-good boy who had his daughter. When he found us, he exploded. He gave the boy a tongue-lashing and then visited his parents. That boy never called again. Another time, my date's car broke down and again Father found us. He retrieved me and left the poor boy on the road with his disabled car. He wouldn't take him home or help him fix it.

Looking back, I don't remember many second dates! Even so, I don't recall feeling rejected. If some boys didn't want to date me enough to deal with Father, they weren't worthy of my concern. I just kept visiting the woods and spending my time there.

When my high-school graduation day arrived, my parents took me to school and attended the ceremony. Then, after I walked down the aisle and received my diploma, we went home. My friends and classmates held graduation parties, but I didn't attend any of them. I needed to be in bed, because early-morning chores awaited me. I missed out on many activities other children and young people enjoyed.

PAIN AND REBELLION

Such things might sound painful, but I didn't feel deprived. Other events did hurt, however. I recall Father buying Christmas gifts for me and then monitoring their use and condition. If I outgrew certain toys but left them in good shape, he took them back and sold them! The same thing happened with other personal items. My parents once bought me a birthstone ring, but when I received my high-school graduation ring, Father took back the birthstone ring and sold it.

I graduated high school in 1970. Doing my best to be the good girl my father desired, I tried to please him by working as a bookkeeper at the local Ford garage. Then I rebelled.

Within a few weeks, I bought a new Mustang Mach 1 with a big engine and started drag-racing at local strips. The feelings I had racing down that quarter-mile strip almost rivaled those of being in the woods. I'd do my own tune-ups and engine work, but again, I was a woman in a man's world. In fact, most of the other racers thought I was all right, but their girlfriends sure didn't. They looked at me like I was a misfit.

I also got married, but it was doomed from the start. I was too young, too headstrong, and I married for all the wrong reasons. As an only child with a stubborn streak and a strict father, my home life seemed a continuous battle. My high school years were unhappy, mentally stressful and filled with physical abuse. I would have married the devil if it meant getting away from Father, who never shied from telling me that he'd never wanted a child. When my chance to escape him came, I jumped at it.

I had known Richard less than three months, but he promised many things, and told Father he would never raise his hand to me. The marriage was not only a bad mistake; it was a long-lasting mistake that dragged out nearly 19 years. It took me 16 of those years to recognize, and then tire of, the false person I had become. Meanwhile, my husband grew to hate my Indian side, and then me.

Even so, we had children, which was not easy for us or for them. That much is certain. The first-born was a son, Richard Ervin, named after his father and my father, Ervin. We named our second child Michelle Judith, and our third-born Rachael Karen.

As the years unfolded in our unhappy marriage, physical problems brought on by stress and my attitude caught up to me. I eventually weighed only 98 pounds and had alarmingly high blood pressure. My doctor finally sat me down one day and said, "You must make a decision, or your body will shut down and you'll probably die. If you get a divorce, you'll stay alive."

I struggled with the decision, knowing how Father felt about divorce. He considered it shameful, a disgrace of the family name. "You made your decision and your bed is made, so accept it," he said.

This time when I went against his wishes, I had no doubts or regrets. When the divorce became final, it only recognized the obvious fact that our family had split at the seams.

TURNING POINT

Meanwhile, I had been approached by the Illinois Department of Conservation about teaching trapping classes. I first declined because I thought it would again put me in a male role, and somehow further shame Father and our family name. The Department of Conservation persisted, however, asking if I would do an animal-skinning demo for young students.

I didn't know it at the time, but my life was about to change. I accepted the invitation and made an important discovery: The students accepted me without question, and found no fault with my role and what I was doing. They surrounded me and asked questions. They eagerly sought my opinion on how to set traps for various animals.

I thought to myself, "This new generation might have a chance. They seem open-minded." Most of the children believed my Indian blood was neat, maybe even awesome. Could something be changing? Could this be the generation Grey Wolf had talked about? Could this new generation be the one whose understanding would ensure the future of hunting and trapping? Were they the ones who would accept Indians, respect our self-pride, and understand the importance of our ways?

Grandfather had told my mother that I, the only child, would live most of my life before finding myself, and my true calling. My greatest strength is my ability to reach children. Once again, Grandfather was right. I was becoming the bridge between the old, the new and our shared future.

PUTTING THE MATCH TO KINDLING

That turn of events was so rewarding. Suddenly my life had a higher purpose. Plus, I eventually found true happiness in my personal life when I married a good man, Herman Kovar. More on him later!

Meanwhile, some problems remained unsolved and forever boiling. Each week, month and year brought different versions of the sad story. My splintered family, the one Herman married into, could have been compared to dry kindling awaiting the match. That match would be my parents' deaths.

Father never figured he would go first. Mother suffered a stroke in 1992, and was confined to a wheelchair. He took care of her the next three years, but when he passed in 1995, Mother she seemed to feel a weight lift from her. She no longer had to answer to Father, his wishes or his rules. I asked if she wanted to sell the farm, but she shook her head and loudly said, "No!"

Her remaining time wasn't without family conflicts involving her grandchildren and me, but her final three months were especially precious, even with the many sad battles and problems surrounding her family. We told old stories and relived special moments, both of us enjoying the freedom we now had in Father's absence. Mother missed him, of course, but she also knew his dark side.

Before long, Mother developed a sore throat, complications arose, and she landed in the hospital. One day, as Herman and I dealt with family problems on Mother's farm, we received a call from the hospital, saying I needed to say my farewells.

Even at the funeral home and during the visitation, I fielded questions about my parents' will. Everyone wanted to ensure they received their share. As happens to all too many families, legal battles ensued over the estate. Inside I was dying, and just wanted to go someplace and hide. The ugliness of those weeks and months will never fade.

Meanwhile, we had problems with my son, Rick, on other fronts, including property rights and maintenance of my parents' farm. We finally had to get the law involved and spend way too much time in court. The upshot is that—as of 2006—more than a decade had passed without a contact with Rick or my middle child, Michelle.

Tears slide down my cheeks when I think about the sadness and torments surrounding my family. Much pain and many fears remain. I guess they always will be there, but we learn to manage or reroute them, and we keep moving forward. Everyday is a gift from the Creator, and it's a gift to be cherished, not wasted.

I continue a loving relationship with my youngest daughter, Rachael Karen Johnson. She moved in with Herman and me for her senior year of high school, and made us so proud by graduating. Sure, we had more than one sleepless night and some differences of opinions, but we worked them out. Rachael now works at an optical service and married one of the eye doctors, Tom Johnson. Tom spoils her rotten and they enjoy special treats that two people in love are entitled to share. We visit and frequently go out for supper together.

One day Rachael Karen and I obtained her Tribal Papers, and got them signed and recorded. She is not ashamed of her Indian blood or of me. But she and I laughingly differ on how best to express our love for animals. Rachael and Tom have a huge pond and feed their catfish, but they don't fish it. When I saw the size of those catfish . . . well, I thought it was part of Cheyenne heaven. But I'm still working on getting to fish there.

Tom helps Rachael deal with the dysfunctional aspects of our family. His soft, easygoing way is always there for her. I sleep a little easier knowing that if I die tomorrow, Rachael will have someone to always help her, just as Herman has always been there for me in my many times of need.

BUILDING BLOCKS

I now realize that every part of my life —whether it brought pain, heartache or joy—was critical in shaping and preparing me for my calling. My foundation was built day by day, year by year, block by block. All those battles had made me stronger. When I began talking to those kids about trapping and hunting, I felt a deep sense of pride I had never before experienced. Once I realized that my purpose in life was to bridge generations and races of people, my self-confidence bloomed.

I guess we never truly graduate school and finish learning until we stop drawing breath. ■

The author's life took a dramatic turn for the better in the mid-1980s, when the Illinois Department of Conservation asked her to teach trapping classes to area youngsters. All her years of running a trap line suddenly proved invaluable. Just as importantly, students accepted her without question and enjoyed learning from her.

4

GRANDFATHER'S SPIRIT

By now you realize my grandfather, Grey Wolf, had a profound impact on my life, even though we shared few years together. His presence helped guide me through many personal struggles, and weaves through all other aspects of my life, from my Cheyenne roots to my modern-day bowhunting tactics.

The author's grandfather, Grey Wolf, has been a lifelong influence on her, even though she only knew him briefly before his death. This old "tin-type" photo is the only picture she has of him. It was taken the day he was assigned to a reservation, given a new name, Abe Dean, and dressed in the white man's clothing.

Just who was Grey Wolf? He was an important man among the Cheyenne, but he was not the chief. He was often called a medicine man, but even that term loses something in translation. True, Grandfather resembled a doctor. If you were wounded, broke your arm or suffered a cut, he could often fix you up. But Grandfather also resembled a priest. If you needed help saying your prayers or performing a religious ceremony, he helped and guided you. Not only that, but he sometimes resembled a psychiatrist. If you needed someone to hear about a problem or to explain a baffling dream, you sought him out and he helped.

Grandfather was 42 when his marriage was arranged with my grandmother, who was 12. A woman—or girl—was seldom asked whom she loved or desired. She was simply told whom she would marry. Along with her went negotiated numbers of skins, horses, buffalo hides and other possessions. As some might say, a woman was more or less property to be bartered.

I mention my grandparents often when visiting classrooms today. I want children to think of the old ones and the way things used to be. Children usually think they lead difficult lives, so I ask them to compare their routines with my grandparents' daily responsibilities. How would today's young girls like to be married to a 42-year-old

The author's maternal grandmother, Nora Bell Dean, was a 12-year-old girl when her marriage to Grey Wolf was arranged. This photo of her was taken in 1935. As Judy writes of the arranged marriage: "Along with her went negotiated numbers of skins, horses, buffalo hides and other possessions."

man of their parents' choosing, and be responsible for gutting, skinning and quartering his deer, and carrying it home? Once everything was home, how would they like to scrape and tan the hide, sew the family's clothes, fetch the water, cook the food, put up the teepee, bear children, take down the teepee, move everything to a new camp, and somehow find time to teach children the ways?

When I ask these questions, most girls look wary and say, "No way."

A SIMPLE LIFE?

Grandfather's life appeared simple. He didn't need a watch to tell time. He ate when hungry and slept when tired. He went hunting when he needed meat or clothes, and Grandmother took it from there. In my grandparents' time, women weren't looked down upon, but they also had little say. The man provided meat and protection for his family. When he finished these tasks and returned to camp, his job was finished.

But the woman's work continued every waking moment. When the warrior brought home a carcass, she just changed jobs. She gutted the animal, skinned it, scraped the hide and dried it. She cooked or dried the meat, and cleaned and saved the bones for making tools, decorations or necklaces. She also saved the hooves or toes for use as bells, glue or rattles.

In short, she used everything from the animal. Nothing went to waste. In contrast, I can't help but think of today's world, where we talk of disposable income, discretionary spending and other terms that define luxury and excess.

As a woman worked, her warrior sat by the fire, boasting of his greatness. Mother often said the braves bragged of their many strengths, but they probably couldn't have boiled water without the women's guidance! I guess an affectionate put-down never goes out of style, no matter your culture.

The only photo I have of Grandfather is an old "tintype," taken the day he was put on the reservation. His black hair was cut short and he wore a suit and tie. His expression showed he was no longer one with the land. Everything he knew was turned upside down or taken away. He was a strong man, but this picture showed him at his weakest moment.

When I visited schools and appeared at speaking engagements decades after his death, I met people who knew Grandfather. They always spoke highly of him, and his knowledge and ways with animals. One man told me how Grandfather saved him and his brother from death when a rabid mule attacked them. The mule was penned up in an old barn, and the boys ventured inside. The mule quickly cornered them against the wooden planks and their cries for help reached Grandfather's ears. He jumped over the rail fence, took off his felt hat, and fought off the mule's attacks with that big-brimmed hat, allowing the boys to escape.

Such stories helped me realize that although Grandfather ruled with a spiritual iron fist, he was also a gentle man who believed animals were his brothers.

Other stories about Grandfather were handed down through the generations. One involved an Arapaho chief who was bitten by a snake near Montana's Powder River. My grandfather and a fellow warrior named Turkey Leg saved him. On another occasion, my mother's sister was helping Grandfather chop wood for the cook-stove when her fingers got in the way of the ax. Three of them were there one second and gone the next. Even a great medicine man couldn't save her fingers in those days, but he prevented infections from setting in and consuming her.

Stories like those filled my memory banks when I was small. At the time, I considered them entertainment, a good way to pass time on a rainy day. With age, though, came the realization that family stories are a bridge to the past that we can travel anytime we want, whether we think about them when alone or share them with our children, so they learn of their great-grandfather and our relations. It is the storyteller's duty to remember those details and pass them along to keep life's bridges in good repair.

LOST BETWEEN WORLDS

Grandfather tried to make it on the reservation, but with seven children and the realization that his life lacked respect, he packed up his wife and children and left. Thick clouds hid the moon that night, dimming its bright light as they escaped. In escaping, however, Grandfather left behind a huge part of himself: He was no longer a medicine man. I heard he sat down one evening and said he was a man without purpose or cause, that he had given up Indian life for the reservation, and then gave that up for the promises of the white man's world, only to realize he belonged in neither.

He apparently fought this inner conflict for years before deciding his time had come. Grandfather felt so alone. He believed he had failed his culture and his family. Finally, one autumn morning, he arose early, walked outside, and listened to the wind and the birds. His rough, dirt-stained right hand slipped into his pocket and pulled out a pistol. A loud shot broke the morning's peace and Grandfather fell dead.

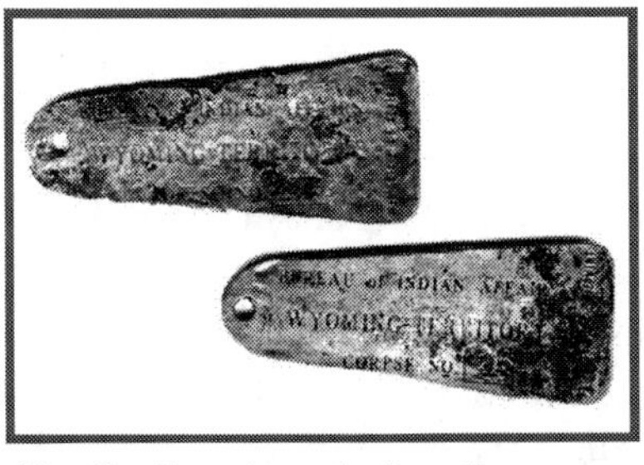

Alice Hamilton, the author's mother, removed these "corpse tags" from a relative before the loved one was buried by the U.S. government's Bureau of Indian Affairs. Removing the tags was against the law, because the BIA recorded the tag numbers, not the names, of Indians buried on the reservation. The Northern Cheyenne, however, believed the corpse tags had to be removed if the person was to enter the after-life free and whole.

Some family members insist he didn't kill himself, but as the feathers fall to Earth, let it be known his gunshot did not scar our family tree. This sad event was the result of a conflict between two worlds, with Grandfather feeling no part of either. He felt such profound loneliness and seemed so out of place with the Earth that feelings of failure overwhelmed him.

I often gaze at my old tintype photo of Grandfather and wonder how he felt the day they cut his hair and put him on the reservation. With the haircut also came a Christian name. Whether he picked the name or was given it remains unproven, but the story goes that he was handed a Bible and told he could no longer use his "savage" name. He apparently thought about it for a long time and finally picked Abraham. Whether he was inspired by the biblical Abraham or Abraham Lincoln, no one knows. All we know with certainty is that he became Abe Dean, and that's the name on his tombstone.

ENDURING PAIN

I share thoughts of Grandfather because I want you to know me better. Some people might not understand why a grandchild still carries a grandparent's pain. But I think pain is part of a precious legacy that goes with the love, joy and pride we pass along to the next generation. It's true that "children are our future," and when they have a full understanding of those who came before, they have a bridge that reaches beyond death, so they are always connected to their loved ones.

Some people might not understand why a grandchild still carries a grandparent's pain. But, do we not also carry and pass along their love, joy and pride?

Grandfather helps explain who I am and what I stand for. I'm a human being with an enduring soul, and I have a heart that's too soft and easily hurt. I trust my heart and listen to its counsel, because another person's spoken or written words are not always true. We risk losing sight of ourselves if we ignore our heart's advice. I might forget some events, names and routine occasions, but I'm forever aware that I'm a Native American, an Indian. Some have even called me a heathen, but I believe in myself and treasure the world around me.

I also respect the land, from which we are all born. I was taught that we're brothers and sisters to all the animals confined with us here on Mother Earth. We need each other and survive together. But I was also taught that, as with all things, our worlds forever change.

For American Indians, our biggest change began when trappers and traders entered our midst. With them came different beliefs, desires and diseases, things for which we had few defenses. Those encounters inevitably brought death to individuals, peoples and entire cultures. My ancestors could not defeat the poxes and fevers that somehow survived long trips across the waters before sweeping across our lands, rubbing out millions.

The author was taught to respect her elders and honor her family. When she looks at old photos, such as this 1952 picture of her mother, Alice Dean Hamilton, left, and her grandmother, Nora Bell Dean, she tries to envision their world. She notes, "Those who don't honor their traditions and repeat their stories burn family bridges."

Those who survived the plagues were soon told they were not human, that they lacked souls and civilization. They were told they must accept Christianity or endure continued punishment for their infractions. As the months turned to years and the years to decades, my people heard of a great white chief who lived in Washington, D.C., and who would punish us without mercy if we didn't obey him and abandon our ways.

UNYIELDING DESIRE

We became confused and angry. We had believed our Great Spirit had provided our land and given the lands across the waters to white people. But we learned there were many whites who were not satisfied with their own lands, for they were filled with wars, disease and people who thirsted to run other people's lives. So great were these whites' desires to escape that they boarded ships and traveled for weeks, even months, to reach our land.

They went so far as to claim that the native people's land was rightfully theirs because of our shortcomings. When we asked why their land wasn't enough—why they couldn't try to fix what they had ruined, rather than try to claim our homelands as their own—their answers made no sense. (And they still don't.)

The whites also brought their priests, holy men and Ten Commandments, and demanded that we follow their teachings. There's a story about an old chief in the Hudson Bay region who went inside his teepee and brought out our 12 Commandments to show everyone. Not only were the whites unimpressed, they became belligerent.

Our confusion and anger deepened. Who would use fear and force to introduce their religion to our world? No God could be that mean. What of my grandfather's great-grandfathers, and all our ancestors before, who never had the opportunity to be baptized Christians? They were innocents. Could they really deserve damnation in Hell because they lived in the wrong time and place? Some of us still can't bring ourselves to believe any God would inflict such cruelty on His children.

We were taught to always respect our elders, and honor our family unit. Has that faith endured in today's world? We move our old folks into nursing homes and

The author visits the Badlands and other Dakota territories from which her people, the Northern Cheyenne, were banished to reservations. She appreciates the region's desolate beauty, but realizes few could survive there for long, especially in winter. This photo shows her at the Wounded Knee gravesite on the Pine Ridge Indian reservation in South Dakota.

explain that our young people don't have time to care for them. Many of today's young people don't honor our traditions or listen to stories of long ago. Their boredom burns the bridges to their grandfathers.

But not all is bad or disappointing. Many people hear the phrase, "from where we come," and recognize them as solid words. As a result, we continue changing. We now dance our sacred dances for everyone, something that was forbidden years ago. We hold our own festivals and councils, and invite everyone to join the celebration of our heritage. We make vases, pots, bowls and other crafts for white people, and many treasure them.

All the while, though, we worry that we might be changing our culture merely to fit the times and someone else's needs. That would be wrong. It would be like the old ones who fought for the land, but ultimately gave in, and discovered their new life actually belonged to someone else, not them. Life will never be simple, will it?

No matter what came before, responsibilities to our children always remain. They must learn from us, and that's a scary thought. Just what are they learning? Do they respect life? Do they respect property? Do they take without thinking, without giving back? What are your answers, and how much responsibility do you take for them, good or bad?

WORDS AND BROKEN BONDS

Grey Wolf's legacy teaches me that words are medicine, too. A few encouraging words can heal, just as a few evil words inflict the power of rattlesnake venom. Once written or spoken, there's no calling back that wound and venom. The effect can disfigure, even kill. On the kinder side, words can offer prayers and carry the soft caress of a mother or the healing wisdom of a doctor or priest. Yes, words can heal wounds and inspire life.

Words on paper can only be as true as the person who wrote them. Unfortunately, my people learned to distrust the written word, and had no faith in the far-away people behind the documents. Treaties became broken promises, which in turn broke hearts, spirits and lives faster than the time it took to write and disregard them.

My people have an unquenchable thirst for life and respect for the animals in our midst. It's difficult for me to explain, but when the huge buffalo herds were slaughtered in the late 1800s, so were the Plains Indians. Our deaths weren't as direct as a bullet to the heart, but severing our food chain had its desired effect. We began to starve and weaken, physically, mentally, spiritually and culturally. When we were taken to reservations, we found ourselves in desolate lands that couldn't sustain us or our way of life. These weren't the sacred Black Hills, where we could perform our rites and dances. We became lost children with no roots and little sustenance.

These days, as I visit the Badlands and other Dakota land, I appreciate their desolate beauty, and realize no one could survive out here for long, especially in winter. But survive we did, and when the government realized it couldn't dispose of us as quickly as intended, it again broke its word, and again took our land. My mother tells of cattle trucks and boxcars arriving and loading up our people as if

People often ask Judy Kovar why she "can't let go" of pain endured by her Northern Cheyenne ancestors. She replies, "Honoring a people's heritage and history requires that we never forget the bad times as well as the good times and age-old traditions, either. I try to give joy and tragedy the same respect." In this photo, the author visits the Little Bighorn battlefield in southeastern Montana. "So many spirits remain," she said.

they were animals going to slaughter. They were allowed only the clothes they wore, abandoning all other belongings and sacred objects.

It's remarkable anyone survived such blows to their spirit and soul. Webster's dictionary defines spirit as "the breath of life," and it defines the soul with words like "specter," "vivacity" and "courage."

I define a soul as a beginning, a guiding hand, a wind or ghost. Breaking the spirit destroys the will to live and all that surrounds it, including the body and soul. The spirit must survive for us to truly live. The two go together.

It sickens me to read how an early priest called American Indians nonhumans and uncivilized. How could anyone describe us in diaries as animals with facial features who somewhat resemble them? Other early immigrants wrote that they struggled to believe their God could have made such creatures as my people! I'm amazed to read such hateful words, especially considering these critics weren't without warts themselves. They had burned people at the stake for so-called witchcraft. They tortured others for being heretics. Later, as they began their march across the North American continent, they sent their dogs into our camps to hunt us down and kill us as if we were varmints. We had held out our hands in friendship, only to have them cut off!

Again, I hear people asking why I can't let go of those terrible injustices. And again, I remind them that honoring a people's heritage and history requires that we never forget the bad times as well as the good times and age-old traditions, either. I try to give joy and tragedy the same respect as I walk through life. ■

5
THE WARRIOR'S ROLE

No matter where we come from, we must honor our heritage and make time to share it with others in hopes they'll appreciate and help preserve it. That responsibility often requires a warrior's pride and perseverance, whether you're a man or woman.

I'll never forget a seminar visit to an intertribal gathering in Owensboro, Kentucky, in October 1994. An anchorwoman at a local television station was doing on-camera interviews, but she didn't come there to learn and relay information I was offering about the Cheyenne people. Nor did she seem interested in the insights of Roger Clinch, a Cherokee storyteller, who was also asked for an interview. I tried telling her of the 75,000 miles I had traveled the previous six months, and the messages I had carried to 129,000 schoolchildren in those travels, but she much preferred the

The author believes her people's future—and maybe the future of bowhunting, too—requires her to reach children wherever she travels. She writes, "Children accept me, my bow and my ways. They look at me and appreciate my heritage, and they listen to their hearts for answers."

sound of her own voice. She was doing a special on "culture," and I soon realized she only wanted us to help her present her views, not ours.

I walked away when I realized I could not reach her. A woman who had just gotten married at this intertribal get-together, grabbed the TV woman and said: "You didn't listen, did you? You should be talking to that woman who is walking away. She is more of a warrior than most men, but you were too busy to listen!"

When I heard about that exchange, I realized I had been called many things in my life, but never a warrior! I felt extremely flattered. I guess I'm a warrior in some sense, because if I'm not out in the woods, I'm at schools, seminars or banquets nearly every day. I'm educating, sometimes fighting, to reach the young ones, hoping my words can be the bridge between conflicting generations and cultures. I'm pleased by the warrior comparison and don't shy from it, realizing my people's future—and maybe the future of bowhunting—means reaching children wherever I travel. Children accept me, my bow and my ways. They look at me and appreciate my heritage, and they listen to their hearts for answers. They leave my presentations with a new awareness. I plant the seed, but it is up to them to help it grow.

That's who I am. I'm with the old ones. I see through their eyes and feel their presence. I fight the modern battles, the ones that require a briefcase packed with paper. The government never seems to change; only the amount of paper! My fight, however, is based on sharing and educating, using tools my ancestors carried: bows, arrows, bone needles and scrapers. Such tools might be old and considered of little use, but the only thing that changed is their purpose, which is now educational. I keep striving to fulfill Grandfather's vision for me as a vital bridge between past and present. My tools help the past improve the future, so listeners know of us and understand our ways. As Grandfather would remind me, "A warrior must do all these things. A warrior must be all things."

Over the years, new generations too easily forget or never learn of the past. They forget the wars, the places and the dates. Or in some cases, they keep trying to win wars they've lost, prolonging their suffering. Only education can fill those voids, so they can know us, the real us—not the poor imitations of us and our stories re-created in scripts by actors on movie screens. We have survived much agony of the heart, mind and body; enduring wars, disease, starvation, forced marches and religious fervor that changed our lives, land and habitat.

RUNNING BATTLES

That's why I still fight the ignorance instilled during past wars, the intolerance persisting in the present, and the prejudice hounding us into the future. I remind people that from 1857 to 1879, the Cheyenne fought a continuous battle with the U.S. Army, its ranks filled with the descendants of Western European immigrants. From Ash Hollow (1855) to Sand Creek (1864), to the Battle of Little Big Horn (1876), many lives were spent. The Cheyenne succumbed after a final battle and the loss of Two Moons and Dull Knife in 1877 and 1878.

The Northern Cheyenne were herded south and combined with Southern

The author clings to every story and photo of her ancestors and relatives. The woman in the dark dress is Standing Water, Judy's great-grandmother. The photo was taken in the early 1900s.

Cheyenne in what is now Oklahoma. In summer 1878, under Dull Knife and Little Wolf, 300 Northern Cheyenne defied the government and started a long march home. It is said 13,000 troops tried to stay them, but they fought and marched until reaching their land, whereupon they laid down their weapons.

The government in Washington immediately ordered them back to Oklahoma. It was the dead of winter when they returned to the reservation and its unheated barracks. The government hoped this would break their fierce pride, but they again broke out January 9, 1879. Sixty-four were killed by the troops, 78 were recaptured, and about 30 escaped.

The two Cheyenne tribes, Northern and Southern, were then placed on separate reservations established on Montana's Tongue River. Today, however, the Southern and Northern Cheyenne retain their unity as a single tribe.

My people, my ancestors, walked this path. Every time Grandfather told that story, our legend, he would instill in me their feelings, their pain, their thirst for life, their search for that piece of the promised creation. Along with stories, Grandfather recounted his visions, or what we now call dreams. His visions foretold the future, including his own death, for he never saw himself growing old. He foretold that my mother would have only one living child, a female, and that her male child would never have a chance at life. He often said, "If the male child would have survived infancy, he would not have survived being a teenager."

He foretold that my mother's only child would be the bridge-building storyteller, bringing joy to others later in her life, well after she was young. He foretold the two worlds I would live in, and the inner conflicts they would bring me. He foretold that I would have the heart of a warrior, and the tongue and mind of a chief; that I would have the woman's touch, but the inner strength of a man. He said I would touch hearts and souls, see truth or deception in a person's eyes, and decipher meaning in an animal's track.

The author feels fortunate to have so many opportunities to touch people with words, instead of bows, guns or other weapons. She believes storytellers hold the memories and souls of many people. These stories are "gifts from the Great Creator, and should never to be ignored, destroyed, abused or lost."

TEACHING WITH WORDS

I've always felt fortunate to have opportunities to touch people with words, instead of bows, guns or other weapons. It's a coup few warriors can match. After all, storytellers hold the memories and souls of many people. Such responsibilities should be honored as gifts from the Great Creator, never to be ignored, destroyed, abused or lost. They must be nourished, protected and preserved. Likewise, each of us receives the gift of life, which we should profoundly cherish and nourish. We're all keepers of these miraculous gifts.

This deep respect for life and the stories that make all lives memorable might explain why people in all cultures explore their roots. Unfortunately, that quest is especially difficult for American Indians. Almost all had their names changed when entering reservations, and those who fled the reservations could never again use those names for fear of being caught and identified. For those who stayed, the Christian names scrubbed their real names from the records, leaving a gap in their history. Complicating the issue further, crooked Indian agents often made up names so the government would allot more meat to them, which led to increased profits through the black market. These gaps in the official record continue to make genealogy searches nearly impossible, leaving a chasm in the heart that can never close.

Maybe that's why I've often fought some of the same battles my grandfather fought, and why I won't quit the journey I've chosen. Then again, I've also experienced many happy moments as pieces of my life's circle came together. I was able to walk away from my first marriage and its false pretense. I was also able to work with Illinois' Department of Conservation, which let me see that children accepted my ways and looked up to me.

Working in that Illinois office also united me with a man who deeply respects the American Indians and our culture. This man eventually placed my hands on the bow and arrow, a tool my ancestors had used for many centuries. He knew I would understand the bow's significance, even though I had never used one until my white man made the introduction. Just as importantly, this man helped me realize I had nothing to prove by hunting with a bow. He knew I was just a woman hunting for her small place within the sacred circle.

STRONG LINKS

When I eventually realized my ability to be the cultural bridge Grandfather envisioned, my link to him strengthened more than I ever thought possible. Mother and I searched family boxes and trunks for items Grandfather owned and used. Mother said if I was going to visit classrooms, and talk to hundreds of children almost every time, I better do it right. I found Grandfather's bow and one of his broken arrow shafts, but soon had to confront a mysterious part of Grandfather's past. As we looked through his belongings, Mother told me "the fire" had destroyed his bone awls and buried his arrowheads in ashes. She said "the fire" had also consumed his handcrafted turkey calls and boxes, as well as the horns from the last buffalo he bow-killed.

I accepted this vague explanation at first, much as I had all my life, maybe because I realized that although "the fire" had taken so much of Grandfather from me, most of it could be replaced. With Mother's memories guiding my efforts, I went to work. Suddenly, though, I began quizzing her about the fire and how it came to be. All my life she had never told me the details, always saying those stories

When the author started discussing her Northern Cheyenne heritage with schoolchildren, she discovered most of her grandfather's belongings had long ago been destroyed. This inspired her to learn how her ancestors built tools, arrows and bows, which generated even more stories to share with children.

could wait until I grew older. That day, I decided I was old enough to hear everything.

Mother said Grandfather was drinking heavily that night and came home very late. Grandmother was strong-willed and refused to allow him into the house in his terrible state. She locked all the doors and windows. Grandfather stood outside and yelled that if he couldn't sleep in the house, then no one could sleep there. He stumbled out to the old barn that housed the mule team and found the oil lantern. He could barely stand up, but he removed the lantern's mantle and splashed its oil onto the house, porch and woodpile. He then took some matches from his pocket and set the house on fire!

The author always draws a crowd when she appears in public wearing her traditional Cheyenne wedding dress made of elk hides. She says the dress's striking beauty always grabs more attention than her blue jeans and tennis shoes!

The two-story house burned to the ground and Grandfather's family escaped with only the clothes they were wearing. The fire destroyed everything, including Grandfather's buffalo horns, bows, arrows, points, bone needles, wooden calls, sacred herbs and roots, everyone's clothes, and Grandfather's buffalo robe. Inscribed on that robe was our family tree. The robe had been handed down from generation to generation, with every important family event painted on it. These milestones included each child's first steps, their ages in moons, their first animal taken, and other events. Everything was written or painted onto the robe, and it's now lost forever.

After Mother recounted this painful night, we resumed our task of restoring some of Grandfather's possessions. That's when Mother said that if I was going to visit schools and universities, I should wear my ancestors' clothes, including a traditional wedding dress. Unfortunately, white elk hide proved hard to find, but we worked putting scraps together for the wedding dress, here and there finding beads from Grandfather's possessions. Next, Mother called people she knew in Ogden, Utah, to secure buffalo-horn beads and enough elk hide for a skirt. The moccasins required buffalo hide, and so we called Arizona. We finished the dress within a few months, and my footwear arrived a few days later. I was now ready for the schools.

NEWFOUND PRIDE

My first big appearance was at Cahokia Mounds State Park during its "Kids Day" event. I had taken part in it the previous year, but had worn blue jeans and tennis shoes. As we approached the park in our van, I knew the test was at hand. When I stepped from the van dressed in that elk-hide dress, a crowd gathered around me and grew steadily larger. That wardrobe helped me become the hit of the two-day event, and everything remains vivid in my memory. At one point, three novice nuns approached and we talked for hours comparing our beliefs. I also talked to eight Japanese businessmen who stopped by. Despite a substantial language barrier, we got our messages across. A local TV crew even filmed part of my talk and program.

When the event concluded, I felt proud. I like to believe Mother did, too. My life was coming together, but would such good times continue?

As I became more involved with the schools and state parks programs, Mother suggested including other items her parents would have worn. My grandfather, for instance, believed that if you wore part of an animal, that simple act made you one with the animal. Wearing turkey feathers gave you the turkey's keen eyesight. Bobcat claws made you swift and sleek. Raccoon fur made you sly and cunning, and bear claws gave you awesome strength. Every animal has a special meaning in our life.

The author's traveling program, "Kovar's Conservation Heritage Seminars," became a reality in the 1990s as schools called to schedule appearances. She believes her grandfather, Grey Wolf, guided her along this storytelling path. In this photo, she shows one of her grandfather's rare arrows, which is fletched with crow feathers attached with glue made from a deer's hoof.

By wearing earrings made from a rattlesnake's rattles, I can be one with him and pass in peace. Why? With both of us wearing rattles, the rattlesnake and I keep track of each other.

People listen with interest as I explain these things and describe our beliefs. When I discuss deer hunting, I try to help everyone understand whitetails, their patterns and what motivates their activities. In my mind, everything connects, but most people don't understand when I say, "Be the animal. Think as it does. My people have a kinship with animals."

I realize that in today's disconnected world of impending deadlines and high technology, not everyone can relate to a time or a people who lived so close to the land. The world we've created relentlessly erodes our hunting instincts, even as I try to renew those instincts in my own generation and younger generations. Those instincts help explain why my people were such expert bowhunters. We put ourselves into the animals' place and became part of their habitat. Modern hunters would do well to learn this approach.

It's important to respect animals, especially when bowhunting whitetails from ground blinds or on stalks. I succeed at both because I let my predatory instincts surface. I don't worry what others might say. It's vital to be yourself, play to your strengths, and hunt for yourself. Don't listen to those who hunt only for the next button to pin on their hat after a successful hunt. Buttons and record-book entries do not make the hunter. It's the spirit dwelling within each of us that counts.

The more talks I gave and the more I connected with my audiences, the more the phone started to ring. Before long, I was taking calls from schools around Indiana, Missouri and Kentucky. After a newspaper article about my presentation appeared in Marion, Illinois, calls came pouring in, and I expanded my presentation topics. I soon developed a program dealing with conservation and American Indians. My traveling program, "Kovar's Conservation Heritage Seminars," was now a reality, not just a dream shared with nighttime shadows.

I have no doubt Grey Wolf somehow guided me along this path as the storytelling warrior. I feel his influence every step of the way. ■

6

BIRTH OF A BOWHUNTER

My seminar series helped me resolve a long-running inner struggle in which I sought that special path Grandfather discussed. I knew this path was meant for a woman who respected wildlife, and who liked to hunt and trap. And I knew this path led through the woods, much like those I knew from my childhood. But finding the path wasn't enough. I also sought the certainty that other hunters and trappers would welcome a woman there.

Judy Kovar has become well known for shooting record-book whitetails, but she also knows the value and importance of shooting does. She arrowed this doe near her Illinois home in 1995. Judy credits her husband, Herman, for steering her into archery, and helping her to realize that many men welcome female archers and bowhunters.

Those wishes were a long time coming, but they started taking shape in 1985-1986 as I worked for the Illinois Department of Conservation at its Wild Turkey Check Station. A tall, dark-haired man entered the station one day, changing my life forever.

Herman and I talk often about that meeting. He tells the story this way:

"I was at a state park, hoping to draw a turkey permit. In the midst of 60 other hunters stood a dark-haired, dark-skinned lady. I asked a friend who she was. He told me she ran the check station, that she hunts turkeys, and that she is a Native American."

Herman has been fascinated with American Indians ever since he first hunted their artifacts in farm fields during his boyhood. When I first saw him, I noticed he stood behind all the other men, just quietly hoping for a permit. He was not outgoing, and only occasionally glanced my way.

Herman drew a permit that day, and turkey season soon followed. As the season progressed, Herman kept returning and we started talking, usually about hunting.

Soon after meeting her future husband, Herman Kovar, in 1986, the author began shooting archery and developed a passion for bowhunting. This photo shows her "flinging arrows" in 1987 with a Martin Dynabow.

He asked about my ability to voice-call turkeys, and he was curious about my Indian heritage.

When our conversations turned to bowhunting, Herman said he had been shooting the bow and arrow since about age 6. His first bow might have been a toy, but it led to a second bow. To this day, several buildings in Granite City, Illinois, still bear marks from his cedar arrows. Herman, you see, was always the "Indian" when he and other boys played.

As Herman and I got acquainted, I began realizing he was special. He said I amazed him, too, and that he was impressed I knew so much about the woods and wildlife. We shared our thoughts on many topics, including white-tailed deer and deer-hunting tactics, as well as my fellow American Indians and the grave injustices they've endured.

When Herman asked if I had ever shot a bow, I had to admit I had not. From that time forward, he felt duty-bound to instill in me his love for the bow and arrow. He bought a new bow and a dozen aluminum shafts, which he fletched for me.

A BOWHUNTER IS BORN

One day Herman showed up at my door with this bow and my special arrows, each fletched with four hot-pink feathers. I was shocked and blurted out that I couldn't shoot one of those things. Herman asked me to come outside, claiming he could have me shooting accurately in 20 minutes. He fulfilled the promise.

When Herman left work early, he usually drove to the farm to see me. When he arrived I was often outside flinging arrows, and doing so with considerable accuracy! Herman was proud of my dedication and growing love for archery. He said I was ahead of the game, because I already knew a lot about the woods and I had the desire to hunt.

For the rest of that first season, Herman stopped at the check station, brought me lunch, and talked about the day's events. When I look back on those early days together, I wonder if I somehow knew my inner conflicts could only be cured by marrying not only Herman, but also the bow and arrow.

But those marriages weren't foregone conclusions. When that mid-1980s turkey season ended, and Herman and I said our good-byes, I thought I would never see him again. Then one day he showed up at my door again.

Much like most city-born bowhunters of his generation, Herman Kovar took up archery and bowhunting on his own. Self-taught, patient and stubborn, Herman turned himself into a proficient archer. He shot this buck in 1986, not long after meeting his future wife.

I kidded him that most women get courted with flowers and candy, but he courted me with a new bow and a dozen arrows. Herman spared no expense getting me started, and he was patient with me. Soon enough he realized he had created a monster. I had found a tool that fit my eager hands. The bow didn't care about my sex, gender, build, shape, skin color, hair color or clothing choices. I was shooting something that felt good, something that gave back exactly what I put into it.

Herman says I'm truly his best friend and partner. He says I'm always there for him when he needs companionship, and that I'm also a good student. He adds that I'm not a bad teacher. Herman tells it this way:

"Judy taught me a lot because she is quite a bowhunter and tracker. She has a knack for seeing things in the woods that most hunters overlook. We pray we share many years together to hunt and enjoy the outdoors."

Like many bowhunters of his generation, Herman picked up the bow on his own, even though he was born and raised in the city. No one put it into his hands. I still find his dedication and determination remarkable for a city-raised man. When he started hunting, he often sat in his tree stand and waited forever for a deer to come along. Meanwhile, he wondered if he would ever find a woman who shared his views and passion for the deer woods. Little did he realize I was living only a few miles away!

GROWING CONFIDENCE

I spent my first bow season hunting whitetails, but decided I would shoot only those with headgear. That was a big mistake, and it made my first few whitetail seasons too dull. I didn't understand that bowhunters can't just step into the woods and arrow record-book bucks.

Eventually I realized I had to develop confidence in my equipment. Without that confidence, it's difficult to succeed in the deer woods. A bow must feel like an extension of your arm, much like fingers are an extension of your hand. Until you develop that confidence, it's difficult for your bow to take its natural place in your hand.

During one of my early bowhunts, I left the house one late afternoon feeling down in the dumps. I had seen a few whitetails come within bow range, but I hadn't released an arrow. Why? I was shaking so hard I couldn't draw my bow! Those encounters made me realize I needed to develop my composure. To remedy the situation, I started shooting varmints and other small game.

Even so, when I entered the woods that one afternoon feeling glum, I knew I needed to take another step before drawing my bow confidently on a whitetail. That next step turned out to be a wild turkey that topped the scales at 27 pounds and swung a beard that stretched 11.5 inches. For some reason, I didn't immediately share my success with Herman. In fact, weeks went by before I told him about it. When I did, he got angry. Why hadn't I called? Didn't I know he would want to take pictures? I told him it had seemed so simple.

The author tried bowhunting for deer soon after becoming a skilled archer, but she was so nervous she couldn't draw her bow when whitetails approached. She turned her attention to small game, and soon after shot her first wild turkey during the fall 1987 archery season. That helped prepare her for success on deer.

Besides, there were bigger gobblers out there. It was no big deal. What did I know! Only later did I realize that first turkey might have been the largest gobbler ever taken in Illinois with a bow and arrow.

Even after arrowing that bird, I didn't take whitetails for granted, but I sure wanted to shoot one more than ever!

Whitetails are not only elusive; they're smart. Each time a deer makes a mistake and survives, it learns from the experience. And if it doesn't learn the lesson, it won't survive much longer. Likewise, we must learn from our mistakes or we'll go home empty-handed. As predators, we must hone our skills and learn how to outwit our quarry, whether it's a deer, bear, turkey or any other species.

After arrowing the gobbler, I thought I was ready for my next big move in deer hunting: tree stands. As events unfolded, I eventually got my first deer with a bow and arrow, but not until I learned the hard way that tree stands aren't for everyone.

Herman had told me tree stands were the only way to bowhunt deer, because whitetails can't see you as well when you're above their line of sight. Plus, I would be above their nose's reach, and I would be able to draw my bow undetected.

I bought a portable tree stand, and Herman took me into the woods to show me how to position the stand and make it safe. Even so, he worried about me and called every night to make sure I had gotten home.

The author arrowed this gobbler during Illinois' 2001 spring turkey season.

INTRO TO TREE STANDS

Maybe he had cause to worry. From the start, I never felt comfortable hunting from a tree stand. Heights and I just don't mesh. On a late October morning, I was hunting from a tree stand overlooking a small cornfield. I had been late reaching the stand, and the slightly frozen ground was growing slick.

Before climbing the tree, I scraped mud from my rubber boots so I wouldn't slip on the tree steps. After clipping my bow to the pull-up rope, I climbed to the platform, grasped the safety rope, and put it around my waist. As I stepped onto the platform, the stand slipped from its once-secure position. I fell backward, with a thousand thoughts flashing through my mind—I had been so careful. I had checked everything. Did the freezing rain overnight make the bark too slick for my stand to grip the tree?—all within a split-second, as I jolted to a stop and a sharp, intense pain seared my chest.

I blacked out a few seconds, but as I regained consciousness I looked around and realized I was hanging upside down about six feet off the ground. I tried to reach for a tree step to right myself, but pain and a dire need for air stopped me. I thought of Herman and my neighbors, but everyone was at work. No one would worry about me all day, and no one would come looking until late evening.

I had to rescue myself, and quickly. I couldn't draw a deep breath, but small gasps seemed to work. I reached again for the tree step, and intense pain again forced me to retreat. I began to panic, but my will to live prevailed. I reached again for the tree step and grabbed it. The pain was almost unbearable as I tried to pull my body up. While maintaining my grip, I rested before fully righting myself. My

The author eventually got her first whitetail with the bow and arrow, this yearling 8-pointer. But as with almost every whitetail since, Judy arrowed it from the ground, not from a tree stand. She learned the hard way that although tree stands might get you above the deer's nose and line of sight, there are safer ways to bowhunt.

eyes seemed to be bursting from their sockets and my lungs refused to work right.

I was scared. My hands trembled with pain, but I had to unhook my safety belt and descend the steps. When I finally felt good old Mother Earth underfoot again, I collapsed on the cold ground and took inventory of my body. I realized I needed to see a doctor, the sooner the better. The trip from my tree and across the cornfield seemed to take forever. Nearly every step invited unconsciousness. I talked to myself and fought to stay awake. When I reached the Bronco I opened the door and fell into the front seat.

My body wanted to surrender to pain and shut down. I don't remember driving to the hospital. How I made it was miraculous. X-rays confirmed my fears: broken ribs. Three of them! After enduring the painful bandaging process, I drove home and waited by the phone for Herman to call. I couldn't wait to give him an earful!

GROUNDED FOR GOOD

That tumble taught me tree stands are not the only way to hunt! I should have known better. I had never felt at ease in the air. I told myself that Indians are not designed to fly, whether from a tree stand or from a seat within an airplane.

That day I decided my body parts, as well as my ego, could stand no further bruising. I haven't climbed up a tree since, and I don't think I've sacrificed anything by staying grounded. ■

7
HUNTIN' TALES

My time as a public servant working at a deer- and turkey-check station in Illinois not only brought Herman and bowhunting into my life, it also produced memories of a far different sort. I discovered that my fellow hunters get themselves into an infinite variety of odd situations, some of which require a game warden's intervention!

Those check-station adventures gave me a sincere appreciation for my colleagues in the Illinois Department of Conservation (DOC). You have to be prepared for almost anything when helping people register deer or turkeys! In fact, when people say real life is stranger than fiction, I nod in agreement and wonder if they, too, once worked as conservation officers or wildlife check-station employees.

The stories that follow all come from my days at the check station. I hope you'll enjoy them as much as I enjoy sharing them.

THE HEADLESS WHITETAIL

On many occasions, I was in charge of the check station, and part of my job was to record the sex and age of each whitetail brought in. One day a guy arrived and handed me the necessary permit and paperwork to register a deer.

After filling out the form, I went outside and headed for his truck. In the back end I saw a hideless, headless and hoofless whitetail. I was stunned, and asked what he had done. It seems that this was his first whitetail, and he wanted it to look its best when he registered it. That was his story, anyway.

He asked me to age it, but I couldn't, of course. There was no head, and therefore, no teeth! I couldn't even identify its sex. I had no choice but to call the game wardens and let them get to the bottom of the man's story. I imagine they did. They're good with such matters.

TWO FOR ONE?

A woman who was gun-hunting in southern Illinois drove into the check station one day with two very small fawns, which were obviously late-borns from midsummer. The trouble was, she only had one antlerless tag.

No problem, she thought. She somehow had the notion that size and weight mattered, and that two tiny fawns would add up to one adult deer. She, too, was proud of herself, until game wardens showed up to discuss the matter.

CIRCUMFERENCE MATTERS, TOO

Other hunters liked to argue with me about the age of their deer. I don't know why, but no one ever thought a deer was younger than my estimate, but plenty of hunters wanted everyone to think they shot an old buck or doe. When my estimate said otherwise, they were loath to believe it.

Granted, I know the tooth-wear deer-aging method and its explanatory charts are just educated estimates, and that it's difficult to pinpoint a deer's age once it's past 5 years old, but the estimates are pretty much slam dunks during the deer's first three years, and especially during the first two years.

Therefore, I'll never forget the guys who came in one day with a yearling buck whose rack had been shot off. There was no mistaking this deer's 18-month-old teeth, but those guys tried with their best silver-tongued blarney to convince me the young buck's antler pedicles had circumferences that measured three to four inches.

No way! Who says only fishermen exaggerate?

When people say real life is stranger than fiction, the author nods in agreement and wonders if they, too, worked as conservation officers or wildlife check-station employees. Her work with the Illinois Department of Conservation often meant setting up information tables and providing educational materials to the public.

ANOTHER FINE MESS

One day, a new Lincoln Town Car pulled into the check station, and a blonde in nylons, high heels, make-up and red-painted, perfectly manicured nails climbed out. Now, I saw hundreds of people pull into that registration station, and I can assure you this lady did not fit the profile of your average deer hunter!

Her appearance was just the first surprise, however. Next, she announced she had killed a whitetail and needed to check it in. This was odd. All of us looked for a deer, but it wasn't tied atop her car and she wasn't pulling a trailer.

"Lady, just where is this whitetail?" I asked. She leaned inside her car and popped the trunk. As we approached and looked inside the trunk, the smell of a gut-shot deer—not yet field-dressed—hit us like a baseball bat. We staggered backward, and two of the checkers did their darnedest not to lose their cookies.

Inside the trunk was a deer lying in at least two gallons of blood and other nasty stuff. We registered her deer and asked what she intended to do with the mess in her trunk.

"Oh, I'll just take a hose to it," she replied.

Somehow, I don't think that mess cleaned up as nicely as the lady driving the car.

While working at an Illinois DOC turkey-registration station, the author met a lot of colorful characters and heard some stories few people would believe. Even so, more than one turkey hunter tried to slip some blarney past her. Most were proud of their story, until a game warden asked to hear it, too.

AND IN THIS CORNER . . .

One morning the area's game wardens set up an observation point overlooking the river bottoms, a spot that let them glass a lot of country.

A shotgun blast soon broke the early morning silence, and the wardens saw a large buck trot into a cut bean field and go down. About 20 minutes later, the hunter appeared to claim his trophy. The wardens watched him lay his gun between the buck's large rack and pull a knife from his backpack.

When the hunter turned back to face the buck, it suddenly returned to life. With the hunter's shotgun still tangled in its antlers, the buck charged him. But instead of sidestepping the buck, the hunter grabbed it around the neck and hung on. He kept stabbing the buck until it fell. Even then, they kept rolling around in the mud, blood and water.

Finally, the buck died and the hunter calmly finished field-dressing his hard-earned trophy. The wardens watched him tag it and start dragging it toward his truck. Later, the wardens dropped by the check station to see if the guy had checked in. The hunter soon arrived and handed me the paperwork. The wardens asked him some questions about the hunt and made other small-talk. Never did the hunter hint at what had occurred.

Finally, the older warden couldn't keep a straight face any longer. The wardens said they had watched the caper through their binoculars, and agreed he was one lucky hunter. That buck could have gored or killed the guy. The hunter's face turned red, and he admitted everything hadn't gone as planned. He just figured no one would have believed his story.

A BEARDED HEN?

The state's wild turkey season also provided many fascinating moments with hunters. I'll never forget the guy who brought in a hen turkey during the spring season. Hens are only legal, of course, when they have a visible beard.

This guy was proud of that bird, but I couldn't see any hint of a beard on the hen.

"Oh yeah, it has a beard," he said. "You have to part them feathers there to see it."

Upon further examination of the bird's breast feathers, I could tell the guy had shot the bird off her nest. Her breast feathers were worn down from going on and off the nest.

Like others before him, this guy was proud of his accomplishment, until the game warden drove up. His enthusiasm then waned. Maybe that's because he knew he couldn't pass himself off as a greenhorn. This veteran had been hunting turkeys more than nine years.

THE COLD CASE

One morning when I arrived to open the check station, a turkey hunter was already there waiting for me. That didn't happen often because I opened at 6:30 a.m. The hunter told me he was there to check in a gobbler he had just shot.

An early-morning success was certainly possible, and I didn't think much of it until I handled the bird. I couldn't help but notice it was stiff and cold. No way did he just take that bird!

As a check-station operator, all I could do was register and weigh the bird, and collect some data. I didn't have the credentials to arrest anyone, and I certainly couldn't judge guilt or innocence, but I was duty-bound to report suspicious situations to game wardens.

Wardens keep in close communication and review registration records. After that, it's up to them how to handle stories that don't add up. I'm guessing they did a little follow-up on this incident.

THE SNAKE CHARMER

In another interesting case, I recall a certain turkey hunter who always carried a few rolls of toilet paper in his fanny pack. After a while, others hunters started complaining about finding white tissue trails in their hunting areas.

When I asked Mr. TP about it, he admitted to the odd practice. Why? Well, he said he had a deathly fear of snakes, and so whenever he set up to call turkeys, he stuffed toilet paper into every nearby hole in the ground so snakes couldn't come out and bite him.

THE WILD TURKEY CHASE

One day a beginning turkey hunter shot a gobbler, but as he approached to pick it up, the gobbler came to life and ran off. The hunter chased after it, but in the process lost his flashlight, mouth calls, gloves and shotgun.

He never caught up with that bird, and eventually gave up and tried to retrace his steps to gather his belongings. The only thing he found was the shotgun. Maybe he lost everything else because he was unfamiliar with the area. It also didn't help that he covered a lot of territory during the futile chase.

CHECK YOUR CALENDAR

A high-school hunter skipped classes one day to hunt turkeys. He got an early start and shot a big gobbler. After lugging it back to his truck and driving the short distance to the check station, he found no one there.

The lad then drove to the nearby park office and asked why the check station wasn't open. He explained he had just shot a big gobbler and wanted to register it. The park ranger called the game warden, and told the boy that someone would be there shortly to help. The young hunter was impressed that everyone responded so quickly to his request.

But when the warden arrived and confirmed a gobbler was lying in the pickup's bed, he walked over to the young hunter and started writing a citation. He then impounded the turkey as evidence.

"Why are you doing this? What did I do wrong?" the boy asked.

The warden asked, "Do you know what today is?"

"Yes," answered the boy.

"You must not," the warden said, "because turkey season ended yesterday!"

THE DEATH MARCH

A farmer decided to try turkey hunting one year, and he had no trouble calling in and shooting a gobbler from his woods. When he was about a quarter-mile from his vehicle, he paused to cross a woven-wire fence. He laid the bird over the fence, but before he could climb over, the gobbler came to life and started staggering around.

Instead of shooting the bird again, the farmer approached and gently tapped it on the opposite side that he wanted it to go. The gobbler moved in the right direction, so the farmer "herded" his prize the entire half-mile to his vehicle before administering a fatal tap, thus saving himself the labor of carrying the gobbler all the way to his vehicle.

AND IN THE OTHER CORNER . . .

On the last day of turkey season, I started compiling the season's totals. As I worked, I paused at times to stare in awe at the worst thunderstorm our area had seen in years. The storm was producing lightning, huge hail and driving winds.

Ten minutes before I was supposed to close, a truck pulled in and a young gentleman got out. He looked ghastly—rain-soaked, muddy head to toe, and wearing a torn and tattered T-shirt.

A truck pulled in and a young gentleman got out. He looked ghastly—rain-soaked, muddy head to toe, and wearing a torn and tattered T-shirt.

As he approached the check-in building with his prize, he pointed out that his monster bird had multiple beards. The gobbler had been active during the storm, gobbling two and three times at each thunderclap. Only when lightning hit nearby did the hunter have a good shot at the bird.

Life offers no guarantees, but it's certainly more pleasurable when we find someone who shares our interests. The author and her husband, Herman, spend as much time together as possible, whether it's practicing archery, bowhunting for whitetails, or scouting and shed-antler hunting each spring. They found this impressive shed in spring 1988, but never got within bow range of the buck during subsequent seasons.

After he shot, he ran to the bird, jumped on it, and hung on for dear life as wounded gobbler spurred and flogged him. The hunter eventually subdued the big bird, and then discovered the gobbler had five separate, measurable beards.

I congratulated him, but couldn't help but wonder why he hadn't finished off the bird with a shotgun blast instead of fighting the bird to the bitter end.

CONCLUSION

I'll always look back on that registration station with fondness. It's interesting how our lives can be changed by something as simple as a job choice. If I hadn't taken that job, I might never have met Herman, launched my educational seminars, and taken up archery and bowhunting. In addition to those life-changing introductions, the check station provided many stories and misadventures to share when discussing how not to handle various hunting situations. ■

8

ARCHERY'S GIFT: A NEW BEGINNING

I married Herman W. Kovar, Sr., in 1990, and we bought a small farm in Jersey County, Illinois. I had the run of the place because Herman worked days as a welder. I spent entire days in our hay barn, smokehouse and 1800s icehouse.

After mowing nearly dawn to dusk one day, I came inside to shower and start supper. I slipped, fell, and smacked my left arm and elbow. The black-and-blue marks eventually faded, but the arm wasn't right. When I tried shooting my bow, it brought terrible pain. Our doctor sent us to St. Louis to see a nerve specialist, who said surgery was my only hope. Trapping and bow season would probably be forbidden that fall.

After my surgery, the doctor said my arm's nerve entrapment was the worst he had ever seen, and he predicted a long recovery. This surgeon knew how much archery meant us because he was a hunter, too.

The arm healed, but the pain persisted every time I picked up my bow and tried to pull it back. When I tried to set traps, I no longer had enough arm strength, and had to find a way to set them by using my feet and body weight.

Herman Kovar shares Judy's belief in honoring, not worshipping, wildlife, before and after its death. The circle of life requires extending one life at the expense of another. Therefore, wildlife must be shown dignity, respect and abiding care.

The pain eventually eased, but I continued to expect more from the arm than what it could do. Even today, I cannot hold the bowstring back for long, and I developed a technique in which I push the bow away from my body with my left arm while drawing. My left arm shakes 24 hours a day, so my shots must now be quick. The longer I hold and aim, the more my accuracy suffers. My shooting style looks like an archer's nightmare, but it works.

I live with the pain, which allows me to better help other bowhunters. When we visit during whitetail exhibits, we discuss bows, equipment and shooting style. It baffles me how many people avoid their bow or give up on it because of physical or mental problems. I say if there is any physical way to pull a bow, do it now. Forget style and form. Just shoot! Who's watching you in the woods, anyway? We hunt because we want to, because it feels good. No one is keeping score!

Bowhunting makes us feel one with Mother Earth, something we experience in our hearts as well as our minds. We see the woodland's animals not only in the best of times, when they're fat, sleek and well fed, but also when they're occasionally sick, starving or diseased.

My people have always honored animals—not worshiped them—before and after their death. Each animal has a just, rightful place in Cheyenne society and culture. In a sense, each animal becomes us when we eat its flesh, and we become the animal. We understand its way of life. Again, it's a full circle, bringing life from the death of another animal. This is how all life revolves, with many saved and nourished by another animal giving its life.

My Indian culture involves all living things. Everything my people needed came from the plains, woods and water—our Mother Earth. Life is sacred to us, cherished as a precious right. When we go afield, we must use natural resources with dignity, respect and abiding care.

All people have the right to decide whether they want to hunt. This is an individual decision and should remain so. Some hunters think that being successful is the way to gain respect in the hunting community. This type of outlook only satisfies selfish reasons. Respect is something you earn. Respect is reserved for people whose acts are unselfish.

PATHS TO GROWTH

None of us has an easy path through life, and we must learn how to look at each joy and setback as another beginning. All things, good and bad, will pass. Whether they improve our lives is up to us, not determined by specific incidents.

My life has often led me along a difficult road, and perhaps I make it more difficult than it has to be by trying to speak not only for myself but for Grandfather and his people. They left a legacy and culture few understand, and I must explain it to help others understand us and accept our beliefs.

I also stand as a woman in two worlds, maybe three. I live by the new ways but yearn for the old. I live in a male's world and pursue an activity dominated by men, so I struggle at times to find my place, my sacred ground. I often pray and make my offerings in town, and then look over my shoulder to see who's watching, who's wondering. I want a little peace and a small place on this Earth.

As you read this book, I hope you'll question your own life and your own world. Consider the possibility that we have all become soft in some ways, and that our children have become entangled in a concrete jungle. We must ask ourselves a

Children need our attention far more than they need toys and technology. If you give a child a bow and arrow, and take the time to teach archery and bowhunting skills, that youngster might now have a lifetime hobby. Herman Kovar, for example, got his first bow when he was five years old and has loved archery ever since.

basic question: What do I need to survive? Can I get by without some of the luxuries and technology I take for granted, things most people in this world—today or long ago—have never seen?

We should also ask ourselves if our ancestors would have approved of us and our society. Our air is polluted, and breathing it makes many people sick. On some days, Herman and I cannot see the other side of the river because of pollution's haze. Is this the world our ancestors passed down to us?

And what are we doing to rescue our children from their tangles? They want to learn, to feel and to experiment. So often they're forbidden to even touch safe things that catch their attention. Do we ever make time to hold it for them, and help them explore?

I ask these questions because I push myself to recognize our many opportunities to make each day, each experience, a new beginning. Maybe that's why I've made my public presentations a hands-on learning program. I remind myself that today's children will someday be making laws and signing our Social Security checks. They, too, need a healthy respect for the land and wildlife to keep their lives in balance.

Think of their future—and yours—the next time you tell a child you don't have time to take them hunting or fishing. They will remember that "no" for a lifetime.

Rest assured, if you make time for them and say "yes," they'll remember that for a lifetime, too.

I can't help but worry about today's children, even as I view them as our best hope for the future. Increasingly, they come from single-parent homes, and they enter our schools and society with behavioral problems, including poor discipline, disrespect and unawareness. No matter what each child's circumstances, they must learn that no one is forever obligated to them, and the sooner they learn to respect others and their property, the more respect they'll receive in return.

THE WOODS & THE BOW

Based on my own experiences growing up in a tough environment, I believe every child requires a place to go, a place to hide, and a place to be one with nature. If a child is as lucky as I was, that special place is a nearby woods. A forest helps children realize what's important. It takes them back to basics, instills respect for nature, and shows them the steps to new beginnings.

Children also need a constructive form of recreation to take their minds off their fears and angers. It must be something fun that they can do with friends, family members or just themselves. Whether it's shooting arrows into a woodland stump or filling a paper target with arrows at a downtown indoor range, youngsters need a bow and arrows in their hands. A great thing about the bow is that it doesn't care if you're male, female, young, old, Cheyenne or Irish-American. No matter who you are, the bow performs for you.

Adults have an obligation to help children as much as possible. The world's physical, moral and spiritual environments can all use cleaning and freshening, but it requires adult leadership. Here, the author talks to Shirley Gelinas of Kwikee Kwiver and her son, Nelson, during a Deer Classic show in Michigan in the early 1990s.

And as with "the old ones," a bow remains patient and forever loyal. It never goes away. The bow waits until the right time and then offers its lessons to those who listen. The bow teaches respect for equipment and for animals. It teaches patience, coordination, timing and balance; as well as lessons on nature and science. A bow can't replace a missing parent, but it can provide some focus and direction as it guides a child through the jungle. With a little help, that bow can teach children of my ancestors and possibly theirs. The bow will clarify its role as an important hunting tool of our past, as well as our present and future.

We all must add positive experiences to our lives and those of others. Without guidance from someone, we all struggle. Adults, especially, have an obligation to help as many children as possible. Everyone can—and must—contribute to make this earth a better place to live. The world's physical, moral and spiritual environments can all use some cleaning and freshening.

Archery is already a popular sport, and hunting with a bow and arrow has long been a way of life. This tool replaced the spear in some cultures and the atlatl in others.

The bow of modern times is more powerful than many of those from times gone by, but the technology in our bows also makes them more accessible to more people than ever before. Not all progress is bad, you see. Some might look at a modern compound bow and find it menacing, but the counterbalance is that it can be shot by anyone, from tots to grandparents.

Life goes on. Pain and happiness, struggles and relaxation, sickness and health; they're all crucial parts of life. Each of us will sometimes think we're not getting our share of the good times. True or not, we must move on and help others along the way. This is how we build self-respect and earn it from others.

RESPECT AND RECOGNITION

I believe in this deeply. You see, it's part of my grandfather's vision for me, and my faith in his vision has brought attention from many.

I was the first woman appointed to the Illinois Trapper Association's Board of Directors. Next, I was the first woman appointed to the Illinois Bowhunter Society's Board of Directors. And next came articles about me in outdoor magazines. Such recognition helped make my name known, but was it ever handed to me? Of course not! No one should expect to receive recognition any other way than through respect from others.

At that point, however, our obligations increase. When Herman and I attend deer expositions and seminars, women often approach me to talk. Some are nervous and watchful. Others approach silently, hand me a piece of paper and walk away without saying a word. Some of their notes tell me that they're proud of me, and my hunting accomplishments. Other notes share a secret: The women who wrote them hunt, too, but they don't want it to be well known. Still other notes tell me that they want to bowhunt, but their husband or boyfriend refuses to include them. When they ask, they're ridiculed, even insulted. They've been told they're "dumb as a box of rocks," or that they "couldn't arrow a deer, anyway."

There are women who have been told it would cost too much to set them up for bowhunting, or whose men buy themselves a new bow and try to hand down their old bows to their "little women." These hand-me-down bows seldom fit a woman, and their draw weights are too heavy. When the woman can't handle such a "gift," the man stands in judgment and makes more fun. Now who's dumb as a box of rocks?

Some women tell me they could never arrow an animal, which is fine. Bowhunting isn't for everyone. But archery can be, so I suggest paper targets. Target archery gets you out there on the range, shooting the bow and enjoying your family. Still, I'm no longer surprised when some of those same women approach the next year and share pictures of their first arrowed whitetail. They're now hooked for life, finally understanding what the guys were talking about and enjoying all these years.

WALK IN THEIR SHOES

In recent years, I often tell the story of "Little Miss Tornado" during my bowhunting seminars. It goes something like this:

You men, you are so proud of yourself and your day out in the deer woods. You come home tired and dirty, but believing everyone wants to hear your stories. You stride into your home, open the kitchen door, and there before you is the tornado herself. While you were gone all day she was cleaning your house, performing the week's errands, and running kids around town. If you're smart, you'll realize conditions are right for a major battle. All that's necessary is a spark.

She takes a closer look. You're still wearing your muddy boots and you've crossed her clean floors. Then she notices fresh deer blood on your pants and hands while she's catching her first good whiff of you. Deer might appreciate the smell of their own urine, but humans—especially women—would rather smell perfume or after-shave.

You didn't just provide the sparks to ignite a fight. You're waving a blowtorch, and the battle is joined!

Trust me, there's a better way. The next time you open that door, imagine that she's accompanying you, not waiting for you. And imagine she's dealing with the

Bowhunting isn't for everyone. The author isn't surprised when a woman tells her she could never shoot an animal, but then later shows photos of a deer she got with her bow. Many people enjoy target shooting with a bow. Once their confidence increases, they get the urge to bowhunt.

Herman Kovar has always made Judy feel welcome in the deer woods and on the archery range. This photo shows them on their wedding day, June 8, 1990, as they wait to "go before the judge" to be married in Jersey County, Illinois.

same mud, the same scent, and the same blood because you took her bowhunting. If you're fighting now, it's because she was right to choose the stand you said was no good. Anyway, you laugh about that while you clean up, heat dinner, and then eat while discussing the day and planning tomorrow's hunt.

By including her, you've given her experiences she's never known before. It might be a familiar experience for you, but for her it's a beginning. She might have seen her first wild turkey or a doe nursing her fawns. Now she better understands your stories. She has felt what your heart has felt. She now knows what happens to the hunter's pounding pulse when a deer approaches and the hunter draws the bow. She no longer wonders why knees weaken and hands tremble when a big buck turns and the bowhunter prepares to shoot.

Just as importantly, you're there to explain her faintness of heart after the shot, and why she must wait minutes or hours to recover the animal. Let her know your thoughts and feelings, your strengths and weaknesses, and what they mean to you. Share these moments! No matter how many you're granted, they'll never be enough.

I'll always remember the young man who approached with a smile and asked to shake my hand. I extended my hand and asked what I had done to deserve the honor. He said he had tried for years to get his wife to try bowhunting. She always refused until she saw some articles about me. After that, she asked him for a bow, and that autumn she started bowhunting. She arrowed a turkey and then a doe. One evening she apologized for all the terrible things she had said over the years about hunting.

I thanked him for his compliments, but explained that I can only share my stories and hope they inspire someone to share the activities I love. The truth is, they should thank themselves, too. They're the ones who went bowhunting together. But I admit it: Such stories make me proud, and confirm that women can enjoy and influence this male-dominated sport.

THE OTHER WOMAN!

Of course, I concede there's another side to this story. Not all women welcome me or shake my hand. Some have accused me of every imaginable sin. Years ago some said I was lying in wait for their men. Others said I was bowhunting just to be around guys. One woman said I should seek counseling because my genes must be messed up. That was interesting. I didn't know psychiatrists could influence a person's genetic makeup.

No amount of talk nor quality of discussion can change such minds. I assure them I go alone because bowhunting record-book whitetails requires the one-on-one approach, not group therapy. I explain that if a woman bowhunts, it's best done separately from her boyfriend or husband. I suppose some men and women hold hands in the tree stand or ground blind, but not me. I guess those who refuse to embrace the woods will never understand the bowhunting spirit, nor the spirits of the old ones who were here before us. The need to hunt and be one with nature and her animals isn't a modern phenomenon, and I certainly didn't create it.

Personally, I believe a predatory instinct dwells within all of us, whether we're old, young, male, female, short, fat, skinny or tall. Each of us channels those instincts differently. Our ancestors knew what was around them in the elements. When my great-grandfather heard a twig snap, he could tell what snapped the twig, its size, and whether it was a threat to him or the family. Today? We seldom pay attention to our surroundings, and when we try, we simply have too many gaps in our comprehension and interpretation.

I'm certainly not Ishi, the last Yahi Indian of northern California, who was found starving and afraid in 1911, uncertain of the two worlds in which he lived. Yet I can identify with him. I have never lived fully among my people, and today often feel alone except for Herman. My storytelling, and my love for archery and bowhunting are all I have.

Like Ishi, I want to share my knowledge of archery, bowhunting and my Cheyenne family, but I want to do so now, before I'm old. I want to fulfill my destiny while I still have the warrior's heart and strength. I feel this urgency, even though I've long treasured every beginning, every new experience, and every path weaving through this circle of life. Maybe it's because none of us can know how many beginnings we'll enjoy.

Webster's dictionary defines "beginning" this way: to take rise; to do the first act; to commence; to enter on. Yes, Herman and I are forever taking new paths, some that lead far from home. But they're paths all warriors must take.

When I close my eyes and listen to gentle rains upon our roof, I recall Grandfather's words: "Leave a legacy for the future." He often told tales of skirmishes, of battles that brought few coups. But each battle survived makes the warrior stronger and wiser.

In my case, whether it's a tree-stand plunge, an accident in my home, a modified shooting style with my bow, or my happy marriage to Herman, all were beginnings and stepping-stones. Whether painful or joyful, they're equally important in creating the path I follow through life. ■

9

THE GROUNDED BOWHUNTER *IT'S JUST MY STYLE*

Most of my bowhunting today relies on ground blinds, or a combination of still-hunting, standing and stalking. I prefer to keep both feet on the ground at all times. That's just my style.

Before proceeding, let's all get on the same page with our definitions. Still-hunting doesn't mean stand-hunting. It means moving slowly, silently and alertly through the woods while looking for quarry. The stalk begins after we spot an animal we want to shoot.

Why do I prefer ground-based bowhunting? I always joke that Indians aren't meant to fly, and I seldom test my comfort level by climbing trees or stepping onto airplanes. In fact, the inspiration behind my ground-based approach was the near-fatal tree-stand accident that landed me in the hospital. As I lay around recuperating from three broken ribs, I decided that if my ancestors could bowhunt whitetails from the ground, this Cheyenne woman could too.

Who says the best way to bowhunt successfully is from a tree stand? These impressive whitetails are proof that it's possible to bag record-book bucks at ground level. The author bagged most of these bucks by stalking them or waiting them out in a ground blind.

THE BLIND APPROACH

Perhaps the best bet for ground-based bowhunters is a good camouflaged blind. Please realize, though, that bowhunting from ground blinds isn't a cinch, and I can't guarantee you'll never get hurt or inconvenienced while bowhunting from one. Some homemade and commercially built ground blinds are frustrations in search of a bowhunter. But if you have a bad experience, don't just chuck the program. Realize some setups won't work and look for ways to improve them.

A well-built ground blind, whether handcrafted or commercially manufactured, can be effective and hunter-friendly. I've enjoyed success by sitting behind or between those big round hay bales now so common in agricultural fields, and have also made a four- or six-bale blind from the smaller standard-shaped bales. The bales block winds on bone-numbing days, they absorb deer-attractant urines sprinkled atop them, and they hide me well when I come to full draw.

If you fashion your own blind or put one in obvious sight in a field, do so before the season or several days before you hunt there. Allow whitetails to get used to it. They're curious animals, but never stupid!

One attribute I appreciate in today's better commercially made ground blinds is the extra room they provide for my shooting stance. You won't find that in a tree stand! Also, most of today's commercial blinds are quick and easy to set up, an important consideration for first-time bowhunters and those of us who don't like tree stands but want flexibility in where we hunt. If you properly place and de-scent these blinds, whitetails accept them. Trust me, they work great unless you make a mistake and educate nearby deer.

When I started bowhunting from camouflaged ground blinds, I bought the Invisiblind from Mark Mueller and used it for three years. It worked well and I always enjoyed bowhunting from it. No matter which blind you choose, however, I can assure you they all require never-ending effort and attention to detail if you're to enjoy consistent success. And that has nothing to do with who makes the blind. In fact, the better I've done from ground blinds, the smarter the whitetails became. Eventually, they seemed to now know my every move. It didn't matter how scent-free I was or how I positioned my blinds. Deer seemed to have a sixth sense that always alerted them to my position.

Finally, I called Keith Beam at Double Bull Blinds and told him my tales of woe. He suggested I try one of his blinds, and reminded me of their seven-second set-up time and easy portability. He also mentioned his blinds' 76-inch shooting diameter, their silent windows and no-wind-flap construction. The more Keith talked, the more I was impressed. But I had one vital request: Had he ever made a Double Bull blind from Scent-Lok material? He said no, but added he was willing to try it.

On the afternoon Keith's new Scent-Lok blind arrived, within 20 minutes I was walking into our farm's persimmon grove.

THE BUSH THAT WASN'T

Remember how I said there's no guarantee you'll never get hurt when hunting from the ground? Well, hear me out.

I settled into my new blind that evening for what I hoped would be a fruitful hunt for a big nontypical buck I had been seeing. Within 10 minutes I had 12 does, that year's fawns, and young bucks feeding past me and entering the cornfield. As each deer passed my other ground blind, they paused to scent-check it. A bit later, I gazed down the ridge and locked onto a buck. It was that big nontypical!

The buck had a long way yet to walk, so I quietly put my arrow back into my bow-quiver and grabbed the camcorder. I wanted a recorded memory of this buck, whether I arrowed him or not. With my camera ready and on pause, I watched the buck work toward me.

Then, out of nowhere, I heard a door slam on a vehicle somewhere in the distance. The noise didn't register at first, but then I realized it had spooked all the deer! Suddenly I heard brush breaking around me and noticed movement. As I turned to look out the blind's right window flap, I saw an adult doe leaping nearby, her front hoofs off the ground, jumping toward the sanctuary of a brush pile. Unfortunately, she was mistaken. The brush pile she targeted for her escape was my new Scent-Lok/Double Bull blind, and I was inside it!

Most of today's commercial blinds, such as the Double Bull, are quick and easy to set up. That's an important consideration for first-time bowhunters and those of us who don't like tree stands but want flexibility in where we hunt.

That doe hit my new blind dead-center, knocking me off my chair! My video camera flew out of my hands, and I fell atop my bow and quiver full of arrows. The side of the blind collapsed just as it's designed to do, and I was mashed into the ground with a layer of blind and a 150-pound doe thrashing around on top of me. The rest of the blind then folded up, trapping me, and the doe, between its fabric and braces. Neither of us was happy about our shared predicament. The doe's bawls were deafening and her hoofs pounded me everywhere, knocking me unconscious.

When I awakened, I noticed the woods were quiet and the doe was no longer around to blame me for her predicament. I crawled out into the evening's fading light and took inventory of my parts. I couldn't see out of my left eye, nor could I feel my nose or teeth. I put my gloved hand to my face, expecting to feel warm blood soaking through the glove's fabric. I was surprised when the glove remained dry. All the while, my forehead was afire. As my gloved hand probed around my left eye, I felt a large part of the eyelid and brow hanging down and resting on my cheekbone.

Still, there was no blood! Suddenly, a wave of nausea washed over me. I fell onto my right knee and found comfort in the strength of a small hickory tree that I clutched on the way down. I felt scared as I took stock of my situation. To reach home and Herman's help I had to drive 28 miles. Could I get there without passing out? I couldn't determine the extent of my injuries. My biggest concern was my vision, but my ribs and legs ached and throbbed from the doe's frantic kicks.

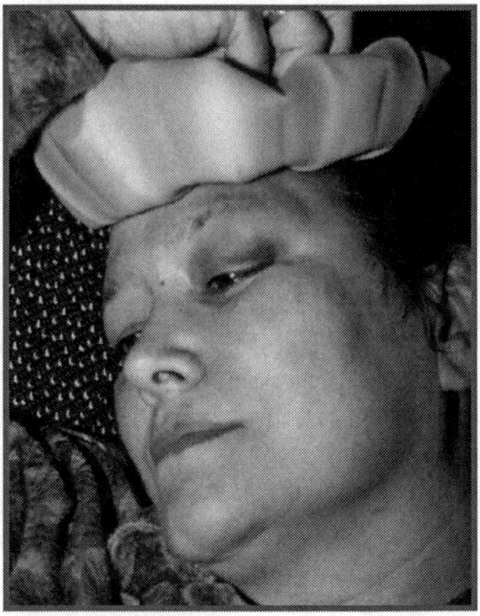

Tree stands require extreme care and respect. One moment of disregard can cripple or kill. Even so, the author knows it's possible to get hurt in a ground blind. Here she nurses bruises, swelling and a broken eyebrow bone after getting run over by a frightened doe. The doe crashed into Judy's ground blind and thrashed around before escaping. The freak accident knocked Judy unconscious and broke three ribs.

Somehow I made it out of the woods, into my vehicle and down the road to home. Herman met me at the garage door and his expression revealed just how bad I looked. I tried to make jokes but he saw no humor in it. I told him I could now give great testimonials for Scent-Lok fabrics and Double Bull blinds. I could vouch for Scent-Lok's motto: "Get Close, Go Undetected." And Double Bull's motto held great irony: "Go out and blindside something." When I realized Herman really wasn't amused, I told him I was just in the wrong place at the wrong time. No one could have anticipated a doe jumping onto my blind, and the blind's location couldn't be faulted either.

Before long I was once again being inspected by a doctor, and then lying around recuperating. My ribs, legs and arms were heavily bruised, and my left-eye socket was fractured, but nothing could be set or put in a cast. My black eye and battered forehead didn't return to their normal color for four weeks.

And here I thought I had put accidents behind me when I abandoned tree stands! So much for finding safety by staying on the ground!

HONING OUR INSTINCTS

Although I'm probably one of the few bowhunters to survive bad accidents in both tree stands and ground blinds, I never considered quitting. I love bowhunting too much. The ground-blind accident was simply a freak situation, something that might happen once in a lifetime.

I remained resolute in learning all I could about deer in order to bowhunt them from the ground. And, again, Grey Wolf guided me. I remembered when I sat upon Grandfather's lap and listened to his wise stories.

"Put yourself in that animal's place; be his shadow and understand his needs," he said.

That's why, when I bowhunt whitetails, I try to smell and think like them. I ask myself questions. If I were a buck, would I jump the fence here? Would I enter the field there? Where would I feel safest and where's my nearest escape and refuge?

How many times have you seen something so unusual that you said, "I wish I had a camera"? The day Judy Kovar climbed into this tree stand was that kind of occasion. She never relaxed for a second when hunting from this stand in 2000, but she did shoot a 15-point nontypical from her perch.

The more I bowhunt, the stronger I believe we must fine-tune our predatory instincts if we're to enjoy success. The deer woods is no place for arrogance. If you walk into the woods believing you're a better bowhunter than a whitetail is a survivor, you'll never amount to much. Deer live in their environment every moment of their existence, so we must respect their well-honed instincts. If you think you're the superior species, all you'll do is further the deer's education every time you encounter them.

The deer woods is no place for arrogance. If you walk into the woods believing you're a better bowhunter than a whitetail is a survivor, you'll never amount to much. Deer live in their environment every moment of their existence, so we must respect their well-honed instincts.

Besides, what makes us think we're superior to whitetails? Many bowhunters start their day right by getting up early. From there, they go downhill, seldom putting themselves in position to score. They get dressed, jump into their vehicle, check the clock and notice they're ahead of schedule. Time for coffee! They stop and walk into the doughnut shop or local cafe. Bacon and eggs are frying on the grill, and those greasy odors soak into their clothes and onto their skin. They wait with their coffee cup while the guy next to them smokes a cigarette. Those odors join the greasy scents on their clothes and skin.

Then they think, as long as they're near a restroom, they might as well use it.

In they go, adding the odors of bleach, disinfectants and other good stuff to those already on their clothes and skin. They pay for their coffee and snacks, walk out and hop into their vehicles.

Now they're running behind, but they look at the gas gauge and see it's low. Better stop at the 24-hour u-pump station. There they stand filling up, adding those fumes to the collection. Then they cross the pavement to pay for their gas, walking through oil, gum, fuel, snuff, transmission fluid, antifreeze and chewing tobacco. They pay for the gas, return to their vehicles and head out to hunt.

Once arriving, they decide they're back on schedule and have time to catch the weather forecast while staying warm inside their vehicles. They keep the engine running and exhaust fumes seep inside, clinging to rubber boots, hunting gear and exterior clothing. Finally, it's time to get going, but as they start into the woods, they realize that coffee wants to get out. They find a small tree or fence post and seconds later the wind is carrying the smell of coffee-tainted urine into the woods they're about to bowhunt.

No wonder the whitetails are getting smarter! They just received a college course on human scent.

The more we think deer won't notice a few mistakes, the more times we'll return from the woods empty-handed. The fact is, whitetails are quick learners because their lives depend on it, and we teach them much of what they know!

LEARNING INSTEAD OF TEACHING

Instead of teaching whitetails much of what they know about us, consider learning something from them and other wildlife. From the time I leave the house, I'm looking around, studying the wind, and noting weather conditions and animal behaviors.

You can learn much by watching other animals and how they're acting. Take note of horses or cows in fields you pass. They can sense a storm's approach, and will try to eat or fill up, because they have no idea how long the storm will last or how long they'll need to hole up. You can bet if they know a storm is coming, so do deer.

Raccoons are another good animal to watch because they also go on a food run the evening before storms. The fact is, most animals go on such a run before storms, but it's cattle and raccoons that we're most likely to notice priming for it.

By paying attention to animals, we can also learn how to move quietly among them. If you like to stalk and still-hunt, your steps are the key to success. I walk a few feet, stop and listen, always looking for antler tips or the flick of an ear. I listen for squirrels as they chatter and argue with deer feeding through the woods.

Seldom do I hunt alongside an obvious trail. Big bucks seldom use these paths. Does, fawns and yearlings do, but mature bucks usually travel parallel to main trails and about halfway down the ridge. That old doe trained them to be wary, just as she trained the females that still follow her deer group up in late fall and winter. Instead of sitting near popular trails, I try to find that funnel where three or four ridges come together, or that small gap between a cornfield and a hayfield. Another good option is staying within view of an active scrape or a well-placed mock scrape.

The more you're aware of the animals around you and how to defeat their senses, the more likely you'll succeed as a ground-based bowhunter. I can't stress how difficult this challenge can be. In fact, I'd say it's never been more difficult than it is now. In my ancestors' time, they could often hunt in full daylight and get deer, sheep, raccoon or wild boar. Wildlife today has turned mostly nocturnal. All of our farming, highways, subdivisions, factories and urban sprawl have changed these animals' behaviors or shoved them out of their original home range entirely.

If you're after mature bucks, it seldom pays to set up near a well-defined deer trail. Does, fawns and yearlings are most likely to use these common paths. It's better to set up within sight of an active scrape or one of your mock scrapes. In this photo, Judy uses an antler to open a mock scrape beneath an overhanging limb.

Mention wild boars—not feral hogs—and most people think of the South. Mention bears and most people think of Western mountains or Northern forests. But in the 1800s, thousands of bears skins and boar hides shipped out of St. Louis every year. Children, and even most adults, find it mind-boggling that so many of North America's grandest animals once lived where they now play and work.

BLENDING IN

Knowing your quarry also means respecting its incredible senses. Although humans have decent eyesight and passable hearing, our sense of smell is almost nonexistent compared to a whitetail's. If only for one day we could scent-check the world with the whitetail's nose! Maybe then we'd better appreciate what we're up against.

To cope with the whitetail's sense of smell, my ancestors dusted or coated their bodies with wood ashes to control their scent. Today's bowhunters have a simpler alternative. I've used Scent-Lok suits almost from the time they came on the market in 1992. That's because I follow Rule No. 1 for bowhunting from the ground: Control your scent!

Scent-trapping camo clothes help me blend into Mother Earth, and that includes putting some thought into my camo choices. If I'm bowhunting a cornfield, I want to look like a cornstalk. You won't find me in there wearing a tree-pattern camo, which would make me look like the biggest, darkest glob in the field. Likewise, I won't wear a cornstalk pattern when bowhunting from inside the woods. I keep more than 10 camo outfits in my closet to match the different habitats and backgrounds I'll encounter most autumns.

When choosing the right outfit, I also evaluate its fabric. When I'm doing nothing except still-hunting and stalking, I stay with wool because it's so forgiving. When briers grab and then let loose of most fabrics, they produce a harsh, tattletale noise. Wool does not. You can get hung up with wool, give a hard tug, and pull through quietly. If you're detected, it's likely your motion, not the sound, that wildlife noticed.

No matter what you wear, it's also important to always look and listen, stop often, and sometimes sit. Take note of what you see and hear as birds, deer, squirrels and other animals move around. Listen to them walk. With whitetails, you'll hear a four-part step as the animal distributes its weight through four legs and hooves. Squirrels run short distances and then stop and dig. Turkeys move and scratch, then move again.

No matter what you wear, it's always important to always look and listen, stop often, and sometimes sit. Take note of what you see and hear as birds, deer, squirrels and other animals move around.

Humans, however, distribute weight through two legs and have a two-part step that goes heel and toe, heel and toe. No other animal has this step, so learn to distinguish it from other footfalls when you're in the woods. Believe me, the animals know our steps! As soon as we enter the woods, they zero in on that unmistakable two-step cadence.

Our natural step makes stalking extremely difficult for some bowhunters, but if you ever hope to succeed in this craft, you must learn to disguise your gait. I've used a type of shuffle with great success. I put my heel down first, which we're used to doing, but then instead of putting down my toes and my full weight, I gently nestle my boot into the leaves and scoot my feet. This makes me sound more like a squirrel.

Unfortunately, this technique doesn't work in ice and snow. When conditions make still-hunting and stalking impossible, I rely on ground blinds, making sure to arrive early. That way the area settles down long before deer start moving.

THE DYING ARTS

As much as I believe in ground blinds, I believe the most satisfying hunting method is still-hunting slowly through the woods and then stalking an animal after I spot it. These methods are fast becoming lost arts because they're hard work, they take a long time, and few bowhunters have the patience and discipline to do them right. Sure, it takes patience to sit and wait in a blind, but I'd argue it requires few

Never lower your guard when bowhunting from the ground. To reduce the likelihood of being picked off by wary whitetails, set up alongside or within a row of large, round hay bales. Better yet, slide your ground blind in among the bales, and/or put out a decoy during the rut to distract deer.

disciplined movements. I assure you it requires far more patience and discipline to place every step just so while constantly inspecting the surroundings. Maintaining such discipline for hours is more than most bowhunters can tolerate.

Stalking an animal is the ultimate challenge, requiring you to move into bow range. You're now on the animal's turf. You're not in a tree stand above the buck's world, waiting for it to approach. You're going to him, doing your best not to alert him! This is a role reversal for nearly all bowhunters. We have the advantage when we're sitting still, listening and watching for a whitetail's approach. When you're still-hunting and stalking, however, that whitetail is listening and watching for you, and wind currents provide nonstop messages.

Never will you be more vulnerable to detection than you are while still-hunting. To succeed, you can never lower your guard or cut corners. You're at a disadvantage, and your only chance of defeating the whitetail's instincts is to remain patient, alert and in tune with conditions around you.

When I'm still-hunting, I usually pick a large tree and stalk it as if it were a deer. Once there, I stand behind or beside it and watch. After a while, if no whitetails appear I move on slowly and easily after picking another tree to stalk. I then set up again. That is the wonder of ground hunting: versatility. You're moving and stand-hunting at the same time.

One of my favorite situations for still-hunting and stalking is an unpicked cornfield.

Where I live in the river bottoms of Illinois, whitetails move into just-tassling corn sometime in June or July, and often live in those cornfields until they're forced out by combines during the autumn harvest. They eat, bed and sleep within those forests of cornstalks.

Slipping down those long rows can be rewarding but also mentally frustrating. The perfect still-hunting and stalking situation for cornfields is a light rain, because all the leaves become soft and quiet. Another good option is dry, windy days when constantly rustling cornstalks neutralize the deer's acute hearing. Either way, choose super-quiet clothing, especially in years when drought turns the leaves into little alarm bells. Just drawing your bow without making major noise can be an accomplishment.

SHARING THE HERITAGE

Still, it can be done, and I've been fortunate to bow-kill several big bucks from the ground. Whether you deliver your arrow from behind a tree, between cornstalks, or through a blind's screened window, bowhunting offers no greater challenge.

By the time I had bow-killed a few deer this way, the Illinois Deer & Turkey Classic shows were up and running. Herman and I enjoy attending these shows, and we couldn't get over the many tremendous bucks on display. Those big trophy whitetails were simply mind-boggling.

An added benefit was that we started meeting new friends and allies for bowhunting at the shows. While attending the 1990 Classic in Springfield, I met M.R. James, editor/founder of Bowhunter magazine and longtime officer of the Pope & Young Club. My fourth record-book whitetail had just been scored, and I was at his booth, hoping to meet him. A tall, gentle-speaking man asked if he could see the photo I held. When I handed it to him, his eyes widened and we started talking. He introduced himself—yes, it was M.R. James—and requested my name, address and phone number. He said he would call when he returned home to Montana, because he wanted to write an article about me, and my ground-based bowhunts.

I gave him the information, but I couldn't help but be skeptical. I had been through this before. I told myself, "When the phone rings and I hear his voice on the other end, then I will believe it."

Soon after Herman and I returned home late Sunday evening, our phone rang. In fact it was now Monday, and the caller was M.R. James!

I'll be forever grateful for the article he wrote about me, and my hunting style. It opened up new doors and brought respect. Little did I know we would become longtime friends, and that he would have a lasting impact on my life.

Because he's a former teacher, M.R. helped me channel my dreams of teaching children the ways of my ancestors, and to share my insights into animals and the thrills of bowhunting. I often call on him when I need things sorted out or someone to cut the cream from atop a proposal. He can be an unflinching critic, but he helps me understand my strengths and weaknesses as a writer and speaker.

The author's ground blind provided a memorable Mother's Day bowhunt for wild turkeys in 2002. Judy arrowed two gobblers from her blind while bowhunting on her Illinois farm.

Speaking of which . . . another important man I met at the Illinois Deer & Turkey Classics also helped change my life. As the mounts of my trophy bucks were being hung up at the show, a friend introduced me to Glenn Helgeland, who owns and operates these shows for his company, Target Communications. As we talked and became acquainted, Glenn asked me to become a seminar speaker. Before long, he had scheduled me for all of his shows, and lined up radio and television interviews to increase interest and attendance.

I was excited by Glenn's invitations and the public recognition. Who wouldn't be? But when I called M.R. to tell him all my good news, he offered advice I've never forgotten:

"This is new to you, but don't do more than you can handle," he said. "When you book too many speaking engagements, and the travel and preparations become a chore, the fun disappears and you burn out. Just be careful and take it slowly."

About the same time M.R. wrote about me in Johnny Boatner's magazine, *International Bowhunter*. For the magazine's cover, he even used a photo of me with a trophy buck I arrowed in Pere Marquette Park along the Illinois River. Johnny and his family also became dear friends in the years that followed.

WHY WE BOWHUNT

If you think arrowing big bucks and receiving national recognition will make you a rich celebrity, let me assure you it seldom happens. I'm not sure why so many hunters think manufacturers write blank checks when you show them big-buck photos, but it's a false assumption. If you don't believe me, just look around and study the record books. Many big deer, elk and bears have been killed in recent years by gun- and bowhunters alike. Now, ask yourself how many of those people have become household names. The fact is, few folks cash in on such accomplishments.

If there's fame in shooting a big deer, it's as fleeting as autumn's colors. And besides, that's not why we bowhunt. When I crawl into my ground blind and prepare for a long sit, I'm there to observe, learn and possibly arrow a deer. My style must work, because I've arrowed many a record-book buck (and never from a tree stand). ■

10

A LEGACY FOR TOMORROW

From the first time I walked into a classroom to share my Cheyenne heritage and bowhunting skills with schoolchildren, I not only enjoyed the experience but believed these educational get-togethers would be my legacy.

Herman and I love meeting children and their teachers, and I do my best to help them comprehend the real world around them, not just the concrete world underfoot. So many children today don't know one animal, bird or plant from another. It is these children I try to reach, and such deficiencies that I try to remedy.

Judy Kovar discusses the bow and arrow with schoolchildren in Chicago. She doesn't try to turn kids into hunters, anglers or trappers. She just wants them to realize these are age-old skills that should be honored.

It's vital that everyone know the animals sharing our planet. I don't care whether children hunt, fish or trap. I just want them to realize these practices are good, time-honored skills rooted in our very beings; I want them to feel a kinship with all wild things.

People are complex, after all, and capable of apparent "contradictions." For instance, farm children raise lambs and calves with loving care, even though they know these animals will be used one day for food. In the same way, hunters and trappers know it's possible to love the animals that also provide their food and clothing. I point out these things because children, especially those in urban areas, are vulnerable to destructive anti-hunting messages. I believe I must try to balance such distorted views of nature and man's role on Earth.

I try to instill in children the importance of conservation, and how they must

When the author speaks to children, she explains why bowhunting and her Cheyenne heritage are both part of her legacy. She wants them to know that the tales she tells about her mother's past aren't made-up stories, and that her white elk-hide wedding dress isn't a costume. They're important parts of her history and theirs.

keep their environment in balance so they are not destroyed by starvation or disease. Hunters are the most well informed conservationists God ever created, and American Indians were conservationists long before government biologists and politicians bestowed such titles!

When I speak to children, I explain why my bowhunting prowess and Cheyenne heritage are both part of my legacy. I want them to know that the tales I tell about my mother's past aren't made-up stories, and that my white elk-hide wedding dress isn't a costume. These are important parts of my history, their own history, and the forces that will shape this land's history long after we're gone.

My topics might jump from Native American lore to bowhunting techniques; from building self-esteem to using the latest archery equipment; and from avoiding drugs and alcohol to preserving our natural predatory instincts.

When we discuss self-esteem, I address the common abuses and temptations of drugs and alcohol, and tie nearly everything back to the importance of maintaining our roots in the outdoors. I tell them with confidence, "The high you get in the woods beats any high you'll get from drugs or alcohol."

I urge them to get into the woods whenever possible. Rather than plop down in the front of the Nintendo or computer, get outside and explore! Be productive. Too many children—whether they live in concrete jungles or in beautiful rural settings—create an indoor world they never escape. I tell them to walk in the woods and feel the ground where bears, buffalo and whitetails once walked, fed and rested. I remind them that many of these creatures still abound in North America, some not far from where the children live.

I also remind them that other people once lived where they now live and attend classes. More than 500 Indian tribes originally inhabited North America. Each tribe was unique, with skills and a culture dictated by its environment. That's very different from today, when people are insulated from their sustaining environment by pavement, plastic and technology that isn't always reliable. Our homes look much the same from West Coast to East Coast, dictated as much by architectural tastes as construction standards that help us survive our varied environments.

Herman watches the children's eyes when I walk into a classroom in my elk-skin dress. Those looks tell him I'm making an impression on every child, and most seem to hang on my every word. They're intrigued by my presence and the way I convey stories and messages. Some of my stories are hundreds of years old but still relate to today's problems. My stories explain why the mole lives in the ground, why the coyote is called the trickster, and why a young brave talks to a rattlesnake. Some of these tales tell of drugs, alcohol and their common abuses.

I realize one person cannot cure the world of these problems. I also believe, however, that one person can make a difference, and we must all do what we can to help while we're here. People must work together to make a better world for ourselves and the generations that follow, and it starts by talking and sharing.

I do not advertise my educational seminars. I rely on word-of-mouth, and it seems to work. During one six-month period, I talked to nearly 130,000 children. All of them get a chance to touch my grandfather's bow and my animal pelts and hides. As they touch and examine these treasures, their mouths express awe, wonder and appreciation.

The mission I've taken on has led me all over the United, allowing me to meet many new and dear friends. I like to think this program will live beyond my time and continue to influence children for generations to come. That's why I still spread

During one six-month period in the 1990s, the author talked to nearly 130,000 schoolchildren around the country. She encourages them to touch her grandfather's bow and the animal pelts and hides. As they touch and examine these treasures, they express awe, wonder and appreciation.

my message whenever possible and give advice to others who believe in these and similar efforts.

Meanwhile, there are other people who spread false messages based on nothing except sheltered, modern interpretations of our here-and-now world. For example, a speaker used to tour Oklahoma with a bear cub and whitetail fawn. The speaker encouraged the children to pet the animals, told them how each animal survives in the woods, and then finished by having the children repeat an oath to never hunt, hurt a wild animal or eat its flesh.

I wonder if such people have ever studied their own history, or looked around most of this world. In many countries today, meat remains scarce and people routinely eat animals we consider pet species, such as dogs and cats. As with our ancestors, most people today have few dietary options. They eat what they can get their hands on.

I also recall a third-grade girl years ago who refused to enter the gym where I spoke because of animal furs I had laid on the tables. She stood back and watched other children walk past, touching them. With a teacher's encouragement and my soft words, we finally got her into the gym so she could hear the program. I felt so sorry for her. Someone had planted false fears in her, tearing her up emotionally. She wanted to touch those pelts and share the experience with her classmates, but she couldn't overcome irrational fears someone instilled in her.

Experiences like that compel me to visit children and show them the hunter's respectful, more realistic views on nature. Maybe G. Fred Asbell of the Pope & Young Club said it best in a letter he wrote to me:

"You have an opportunity, perhaps a responsibility, and it all lies before you."

ADDRESSING OTHER FEARS

My appearances often remind me of many huge tasks remaining. I have walked into auditoriums of 500 children and been greeted by Indian war cries. I calmly tell them they have been watching too much TV, and too many shoot 'em up Westerns.

Once, while addressing a group of wide-eyed preschoolers sitting before me, I called on a small-framed, blond-haired, blue-eyed boy.

He asked, "Are you a real Indian?" I replied that I was.

"But aren't you supposed to have red skin. They did call you redskin. Your skin isn't red."

I assured him I was as real an Indian as he would find these days.

He tilted his head, looked at me, and said, "But that can't be."

I asked why.

He quickly replied, "Because you're all dead. There are no more Indians. John Wayne shot all of you!"

I told him I hated to ruin his day, but that many of us are very much alive, including me.

I've also had children leave the room or walk restlessly around the gym because they thought Indians were bad and might harm them. They were afraid of

The author explains how the Northern Cheyenne and other Native Americans used animal bones for an assortment of tools, including bone scrapers, hoes, rakes and awls.

me, even though we had never before met. One time a little girl asked the color of my blood. I told her it's the same as hers. She simply answered, "My mother says you're dirty."

Such comments stump me. How can I ever change a little girl's mind? How can she learn the truth? If she believes what she has been taught, including that her mother is always right, what chance do I have of getting her to look beyond her prejudices?

Other questions are deeper and more thought provoking, but still don't lend themselves to quick, easy answers. For instance, high school girls have asked why Indian women didn't strike back against our men when they demeaned women or were cruel to us?

On a lighter note, children sometimes touch my skin and face as if I'm going to break. Or maybe they think I'm part of a dream and will soon disappear. They touch my hair and seem fascinated with its blackness and texture. One young child followed me around with a pair of scissors most of the day at his Catholic school, intending to cut off some of my hair to take home. Sister Michelle tried to set him straight, but every time I turned around he was still there!

Although I'm sometimes amazed or saddened by the children's questions, most of their queries come from sincere curiosity. I've been asked what Indian women wear under their dresses, what I wear under mine, and what I sleep in. Teenage girls have asked what ancestral Indian women used for protection when menstruating. And what did Indians use as baby diapers?

When visiting schools to speak, the author recalls her own difficult times in the classroom when she was young. Those memories help her connect with children and she tries to boost their self-esteem. She loves their many innocent questions, and shares stories that teach them about animals and nature's world.

PEER PRESSURES, LONELY HOMES

Each time I visit schools, I also am reminded of my own childhood struggles in school. I forget how often I've see children single out someone with a different skin color, religion or nationality.

I once gave an outdoor presentation to a fourth-grade group that included an obese black child. The others would not let him sit at their table, so he ate his lunch alone as I spoke. Children can be so cruel to each other. I always tell them that just because Tommy doesn't have air-pillow Reeboks or Lisa doesn't use hair spray to cement her tresses into pink spikes, those aren't reasons for other kids to refuse to play with them.

I guess there has always been peer pressure, but these small groups can rip at young people's self-confidence and eat away at their self-esteem. As adults, we want children to choose the right path as they try to fit in, but too many fall between the cracks and into the dirt. We want children to come to terms with others and themselves, but even as I advise such things, my childhood memories remind me that my own battles aren't yet over. Maybe that is why children tug at our heartstrings so. Their struggles are so much more obvious than an adult's.

And the things children say! A young girl, maybe 12, once approached me at a school, clutching a tattered photo in her small hands. She asked me my full name and I told her. Then she asked if I had ever been in this town before. I told her the name sounded familiar and that I probably had. She opened her hands to reveal a photo that showed a young woman with the same color and hairstyle as mine. I said it was a nice photo and gave it back. She then looked into my eyes and asked, "Can you be my mother? This is your photo isn't it? This is you a few years ago. This is the only photo I have of my mother and it looks like you. I promise to be a good daughter and make you proud. Can I be your daughter?"

My heart sank and a sick feeling overcame me. Here stood a young girl so full of life, hoping I would say "yes" to her plea. I looked for a teacher, someone, anyone, to help as I talked to her. I didn't want her to start crying. Finally I took the girl's hand and explained that the photo wasn't me, and that I was telling the truth. I said I had children of my own and three from Herman's side. She listened and said she just wanted a mother so badly, and hoped that her mother would have been like me.

My heart ached. When her class left the gymnasium I told her teachers and guidance counselors of her cries for help. That evening I walked into the house and into Herman's arms and cried. It seemed every time I closed my eyes I saw her. That girl's pleas, and her eyes, will haunt me forever.

On another occasion, a boy in southern Illinois asked what I thought of hanging the mounts of trophy bucks on a wall. I told him we must respect animals in life and death. I said a buck was a king, the master of the woods and the whitetail's world. I said bowhunters must fool the buck's eyes, nose and ears; and the day I arrow a special buck is forever exceptional. I honor the buck by entering him in our record books. I said I don't enter the buck to honor me, the hunter; I entered him to honor the animal.

I also told the boy that every time I look up and view the mounted buck, I relive the moment. I could see the buck walking down the path, see him stop and munch on a few acorns, and watch as his nose tested the wind and his eyes searched his back-trail. I could see him when we came face to face not 20 yards away, and I knew the moment of truth was near. I told him that for every deer head that hangs on our wall, I relive a story. In reliving the story, I honor the animal, just as my ancestors did.

The boy listened with interest, and then looked up at me and said, "No one ever explained it to me like that before. It's all right to hunt, isn't it?"

A teenage girl asked me why I hunt and why with a bow. I told her that sometimes things here on Mother Earth can get bad, even go terribly wrong. But whether we're enjoying good times or enduring the bad, people need to get away from their manmade world and spend time in the woods. We can always go into the woods to find peace and quiet.

Why did I choose the bow for hunting? One reason is Herman. And, of course, the bow and arrow were my ancestors' weapons. I also said I find more solitude in the deer woods during bow season, unlike gun season, when so many hunters are out there, too. I think bowhunting puts us one-on-one with nature and her animals, which makes me feel at ease.

CREATIVE COMMUNICATION

In Alaska, I once visited a junior high school where few of the teenagers could speak English. They had come from all corners of the world, including Brazil, Vietnam, Thailand, Russia, England and France. Their parents were working on nearby pipelines or oil rigs. They had been uprooted and sent to this place, where they were fighting to survive and to understand our ways and language.

Once we found a way to communicate with each other, they really enjoyed the animals, hides and pelts. Until that point, many didn't know a white-tailed deer from a bison. How did we connect? With a teacher's help, I used a picture dictionary and hunting magazines to help them identify each animal before they touched its hide or pelt. After seeing pictures of these animals, they talked among themselves in their own languages and compared the animals with those of their homelands.

Two weeks after I returned home from that trip, a package arrived from Alaska. Enclosed were letters from the children, both in English and in their native languages. Their heartfelt letters touched me profoundly.

In other cases, I have walked into gymnasiums full of hundreds of students,

While visiting a school in Alaska, Judy brought along the hide of a javelina from the American Southwest. The children didn't know such animals existed, and listened spellbound as she described the region and the habitat in which javelinas live and thrive.

and later heard this had been only their third assembly in three years. Why? The last time they held one, two students were stabbed and one died. I have also received police escorts in and out of schools because the neighborhoods were bad and a lone person was almost sure to be attacked. And I have visited other places where students picked up aluminum cans for a month to help pay for my gas money so that I could visit their school.

I have also gone to schools where my display was in the library under the watchful eyes of parents and teachers. Yet by day's end, I was missing two bone needles, an awl and an entire tanned deer hide. How one of those schoolchildren could hide an entire deerskin under their shirt remains a mystery!

Young men from street gangs have talked to me of the color of my blood, and why they fight for their colors—be it the color of their clothes, skin or blood. They compared their fighting to that of my ancestors, boasting about spilling their blood. I said there's a fine line dividing both, explaining that clothes and colors don't change the person inside. I told them they have minds of their own, and to use their brains to ignore those who might twist words and speak falsehoods. The reasons for most fights are usually quickly forgotten, which suggests they aren't worth the blood spilled or lives ruined.

Small children have asked me about scalping and whether I believe in it. I explain to them that scalping came from English immigrants, who paid bounties for a piece of human hair. I said early trappers and traders brought whiskey—firewater—and gave it to us for free until, as with any drug, we became addicted. My ancestors wanted more free firewater, but the immigrants refused. We asked how do we get this whiskey, this firewater? They explained that for a piece of human hair, my people would receive money, and with this money we could buy firewater. So we took scalps, received our payments, bought the firewater, and became addicted to the white man's poisons. It soon became a never-ending circle of misery and death, turning us away from our circle of life.

That piece of history reminded me of a recent visit with my family doctor and a story of his intern years in medical school. He had visited various reservations and studied American Indians closely. The first settlers thought it was funny to see a drunken Indian, and wondered why it took so little to make us drunk. My doctor also said American Indians often suffer from high blood pressure and stress-related illnesses, all related to our genetic dispositions.

I too, have tried this firewater. Once. My 21st birthday was a special event, and I discovered that my system doesn't handle alcohol at all. I was sick three days and hallucinating. Grandfather had warned me, but I had thought his story was only a tall tale. Ever since that day I have not touched alcohol, but I guess I had to learn firsthand that Grandfather was right again. Alcohol consumption just doesn't make sense, especially when you're sick on the outside and inside.

I discuss these things during my visits because I want children to know about the evils of drugs and alcohol. These things will always remain our enemies. I also tell my stories about my people and how we treat each other because I firmly

In addition to teaching kids about animals, bowhunting and the natural world, the author also discusses problems created by drugs, alcohol, prejudice and intolerance.

believe there's more hope on that front. But I know it won't happen in one or two generations. All things today are not fair and right. In some areas it's still possible for us to be stopped at a restaurant's front door and told no tables are available. Some establishments also find ways to keep us out of their restrooms.

That's why I ask children to work for these changes, for I will probably never see a total change in my lifetime. I try to get them to look ahead, to see things as they are, and to think for themselves. They should not allow others to dictate what course their lives will take. I want them to remember my ancestors, their ancestors, and the price many people paid and others demanded for their beliefs.

It saddens me when children and teenagers still see movies and TV shows that portray my people as inferior, bloodthirsty savages. I again explain that a piece of paper can lie, and that anyone can write anything they want on it. But just because someone writes words or utters thoughts does not make those words true. A person must be as good as his words. If not, he lives amid false hopes and misdeeds, and dishonors himself and those who embrace his lies and insults. ■

11

RECORD-BOOK WHITETAILS

Of the nine record-book whitetails I've taken with a bow as of 2006, each was different and was hunted as such. That's one of the great things about bowhunting: Every trip into the woods offers new experiences, and every bowhunt becomes its own story and adventure. I could write an entire chapter on each of these bucks, but instead I decided to relive my hunts for my first four record-book entries. I guess they remain especially memorable for me all these years later.

A few days after falling from a tree stand and breaking her ribs, and still in much pain, the author set up in a hay-bale blind and arrowed this 10-pointer, her first Pope & Young buck. The buck netted 140-6/8 on the P&Y Club's scoring system.

After dropping her first Pope & Young buck, Judy watched two other bucks charge out of the woods to see what was going on. They stood within bow range, snorting, stomping around and making a commotion.

HAY BALES AND BROKEN RIBS

I arrowed my first record-book whitetail soon after I fell from a tree stand and broke my ribs. I wasn't sure I could pull the bow back when I went out that day, but there I was in my hay-bale blind, determined to make the best of it.

I soon spotted several does munching on acorns up on the nearby ridge, working their way toward the picked cornfield where I waited. They entered the field and had been feeding a long time before a buck appeared and jumped the woven-wire fence to join them. I was watching him, hoping to get a shot before he jumped the fence, but he walked too fast and leaped the fence before I could get ready. Before long, he again came into range.

Then came the moment, those special few seconds, when we made eye contact and I released the arrow. My shot spined him, but he didn't go down immediately, so I shot a second arrow into him. When he went down, two other bucks charged from the woods. One was a nontypical I had seen in the cornfield before. They stood on the other side of the fence, snorting and blowing. They were so close I could have shot either of them.

HILLTOP RACE; ACING A SHOT

My second record-book buck was an 11-point nontypical that scored 175 inches. I got a late start that day in early December, first taking my children to school and then reaching the cut cornfield around 10 a.m. I spotted him alone in the corn stubble, feeding toward me. The buck, however, noticed my movements and started to leave.

The race was on to see which of us could reach the top of the nearby ridge first! As I ran, I struggled to maintain my balance while jumping over the rows of picked corn. Cold air stung my lungs as I sucked in big gulps. I remember calling to Grandfather to help me, and my legs.

Suddenly the buck and I were face to face on the ridge. That moment came and went in the flicker of a bird's wing, and then the buck whirled and retreated down a logging road, me running after him again. The buck soon stopped to check his back-trail and wind. He had no idea where I had gone, and I had run past him on a parallel logging road nearby, unsure where he had gone. My eyes searched the two paths where they merged into one. I looked for tracks, broken limbs, and any other sign he had passed by, but found none. Against all my teachings I walked back down the path where I had last seen him, listening and searching the timber.

Then, not 20 feet off the trial, I spotted the buck behind a small, forked ash tree! I drew my bow,

Who says a bowhunter can't keep up with a spooked whitetail? Judy spotted this monstrous 175-inch buck in a cut cornfield, and then trotted after it when it fled into the woods.

The author poses with her largest buck ever. She shot her big 175-inch nontypical after running after it into the woods, and then sneaking within 20 feet without spooking it.

sized up the shot one more time, and released my arrow. The ash tree was in my arrow's path, but I laced the arrow between its forks. My pink fletching guided the arrow through the small opening and it disappeared into the buck. He took off, but I soon found him crumpled in a deep ravine. He apparently died in midair while jumping the ditch. To extract the buck from the ravine we needed our tractor, logging chains, and help from our neighbor.

I remember Father's harsh words as I protected the buck's rack and head in my arms: "Them antlers don't boil worth a damn. What the hell are you holding them for?" I looked at him and replied, "Because they'll look good on the wall."

ANSWERING THE BELL

Here's another look at the author's impressive nontypical buck. Chalk up another big whitetail for Judy and her Martin Dynabow. She became well known for her arrows' hot-pink feathers and tracers.

My third record-book whitetail was an 11-point buck that took on a 22-pointer in a dramatic fight that unfolded in our farm pond. I was sitting in an old permanent stand within a fallen treetop one evening, hoping for a crack at a huge nontypical buck I had spotted. I saw the huge buck come over our pond's dry dam accompanied by 10 does and fawns. What a sight! I watched as he lorded over them and checked them out. Next, a younger buck appeared from the edge of the ridge, and I could see it sported a wide 11-point rack. The intruder trotted along the ridge, quickly closing the distance. When he laid his ears back I knew what would follow.

The does suddenly scattered along the edge of the woods, like bystanders scurrying from a high-noon duel. When the big nontypical noticed the younger challenger, he moved into the first two picked rows of corn in front of the pond. The challenger kept his head down and his ears laid back. He grunted now and then, and suddenly charged when he got within about seven feet of the nontypical. The clash of those massive racks coming together sent shivers down my spine. The two bucks stumbled toward the pond, and when they hit the water its surface boiled all around them. Water erupted four to five feet into the air, and blood spurted from the nontypical's mouth. I thought he might be in trouble.

About that time the nontypical lost his footing in the deep water and went under. It seemed like forever before he resurfaced, and then both deer climbed out

This 1991 photo shows Judy Kovar with her first four Pope & Young bucks. She shot them in consecutive years from 1987 through 1990. The photo accompanied an article in Bowhunter magazine when its editor and co-founder, M.R. James, wrote about her accomplishments for the first time.

of the pond and back to the field's edge. The 11-pointer then lost his footing and fell, and the nontypical struck quickly, lowering his head and driving his antlers into the antagonist's midsection, drawing blood. The challenger regained his footing, but then faltered as he pushed the nontypical. He fell again, this time between the corn rows. Blood now mixed with his saliva, and his breathing became raspy and labored.

The big nontypical turned, looked at his harem and then back to the downed buck. He threw his head back and shook himself. He seemed to say, "Hey, baby, here I am. I won!" I looked at the does and then at him, studying his antlers more carefully. I counted 22 points and main beams as thick as a soda can. I thought of the does now within his grasp and began to dream: If this buck bred most of those does, and the mature does all had twins, and the young does all had singletons, just think of all the little mega-bucks running around in a few years!

The buck slowly walked over to the harem and retreated with them back into the woods. I again looked at the 11-pointer sprawled in the corn. He remained on the ground, but was now looking around. Still, he looked beaten and worn out. I had laid my rattling antlers at my feet when the battle began. I now hit them gently with my left foot, and then tapped them again. I thought the stricken buck might have enough juice to look my way, but I never expected him to get up and charge toward me. The next thing I knew, he was headed my way on a dead run!

If I was going to get a shot, I had to be quick with a plan. As the buck ran past my stand, I kicked the rattling antlers once again. The buck hit the brakes and I drew my bow. Good luck and the hunting spirits united as one, and I released my arrow the instant he stopped. My arrow struck where his neck met the shoulder, breaking his spine. He flipped over in the muddy ground, again landing between rows of corn.

I got the shakes as I stood looking at him. I then walked slowly toward the buck and tapped him with my bow. My mind now reeled! He was down and beaten, his neck broken, yet he still wanted to fight! After finishing him off, I reflected on everything I had just witnessed.

His battle with the 22-pointer had gotten him so riled up and focused on fighting that he couldn't think clearly when I kicked my rattling horns. He acted like a boxer reflexively answering the bell for the next round. He might have been down, but he would not be counted out! I also felt privileged. How many bowhunters have ever seen an actual buck brawl, not just a little patty-cake sparring contest? I thought long and hard about that big nontypical, hoping I would get another crack at him someday, but it never happened. My consolation was contemplating all those little mega-bucks that might be around in subsequent years.

A BITTERSWEET ENDING

My fourth record-book whitetail was a heartbreaker, but here's the story: Herman and I drew permits to hunt Illinois' Pere Marquette Park, which borders the Illinois and Mississippi rivers. Herman was more familiar with the park than I was, and when I got frustrated with an uncooperative buck I spotted three straight days, Herman let me take over his spot on a ridgeline. He wasn't that keen on hunting inside the park anyway, and wanted to chase some bucks he had seen on his private property nearby.

Even though my rattling and calling had gotten the same buck's attention three straight days, it never approached close enough for a shot. I only had time for a five-day hunt, which contributed to my aggravation. Herman joined me on one occasion to double-team the buck, but that didn't work either. The buck seemed to be teasing me. Each time it hung up 30 to 40 yards away, almost as if it knew I didn't feel comfortable shooting that distance. He then angrily tore into young trees, shredding their trunks with his big antlers.

The fact that I was pulling him into view told me I was doing something right, but I needed him closer. For my next trick, I decided to hang a tarsal gland above his scrape and soak the scrape with another buck's urine. Those tasks complete, I prepared a setup less than 10 yards away from the scrape. I would go for broke.

Unfortunately, when I returned the next morning I was a bit late. As I neared the site, I saw the buck work the scrape and then depart. I still-hunted my way around the scrape, hoping he was nearby, but finally gave up and returned to my setup 10 yards downwind of his scrape. I again checked the wind and settled in for the morning. When I picked up the rattling antlers and softly clanked them together, I heard a buck nearby. It was him! He ran straight to the scrape I had doctored, and stuck his nose into it.

I quickly drew my bow and shot him from seven yards away. When the arrow

The author poses in this photo with her third Pope and Young buck. She arrowed this 11-pointer in December 1989 while sitting in a blind built within a fallen treetop.

hit, he was so caught up in his scrape frenzy that he whirled and faced me, saliva dripping from his mouth. His neck muscles were tense, his front legs locked. Maybe he thought another buck had hooked him with an antler.

My arrow was sticking out both sides of the buck, and I was sticking out both sides of a three-inch thick dogwood tree that shielded me from the angry buck! We were basically face-to-face, and I thought I was about to be shredded like just another sapling. But then he realized I wasn't a rival buck and ran off.

I didn't know it then, but that buck's run would take me on a two-week hunt for his remains. I had shot him too far back, hitting his liver.

I went to the park office and called Herman, his son Jeff, and some other bowhunters and park personnel, including Richard Neimeyer. Richard found pieces of liver on a woven-wire fence and blood on the leaves. Unfortunately, we misread the sign at the fence and followed the wrong trail, taking us far from the buck's body. When we didn't find him on that initial search, I continued hunting for his remains every day in the days and weeks that followed. I had to find him, and I would not hunt another deer because I was certain my shot had been lethal.

Richard also hunted for my buck after work and on weekends, and he found some remains, but they were from a smaller buck. After Herman and Jeff went hunting one day, I again returned to the park with a different plan. Instead of climbing over the woven-wire fence and following the trail we assumed the buck had followed, I followed the fence line itself. Why? I remembered how the leaves were disturbed in a huge circle in front of it. We had already looked everywhere else by now, so I reasoned that maybe the buck had circled and turned in front of the fence, not wanting to jump it in his condition.

I began finding hair and toe bones, and after going uphill a ways, I saw the outline of an antler under a fallen tree. I had found my buck, with the middle part of my Easton shaft still within the back half of his body.

Herman did his best to ease my bittersweet feelings. "Few people would have stayed on the trail like you did," he said. "Others would have given up long ago!"

Again, luck and the spirits were with me when I decided to follow the fence line. I guess Father might have been right about something. Although it's true that antlers do not boil worth a damn, neither do they rot. They looked great when I put them on our wall at home, where they pay nonstop tribute to the buck that carried them. ■

Judy Kovar's Pope & Young Whitetails

Deer	Kill Date	Score/ Antler Points	County	State	Hunting Method
Typical Whitetail	10/27/2005	136; 10 pts.	Jersey	Illinois	Blind, decoy, scent
Typical Whitetail	10/30/2004	145-1/8; 8 pts.	Jersey	Illinois	Spot & Stalk, scent
Typical Whitetail	11/6/2002	146; 11 pts.	Jersey	Illinois	Sniper suit, scent, decoy
Typical Whitetail	11/10/1997	128-3/8; 8 pts.	Calhoun	Illinois	Blind, calling, scent, decoy
Typical Whitetail	11/27/1993	140-2/8; 9 pts.	Jersey	Illinois	Calling, stalking
Typical Whitetail	11/8/1990	148-2/8; 12 pts.	Jersey	Illinois	Stalking, rattling
Typical Whitetail	12/29/1989	147-4/8; 11 pts.	Jersey	Illinois	Blind in a fallen treetop
Nontypical Whitetail	12/6/1988	175; 11 pts.	Jersey	Illinois	Stalking, rattling
Typical Whitetail	11/7/1987	140-6/8; 10 pts.	Jersey	Illinois	Hay-bale blind

12

FACING CHALLENGES, ARROWING ADVERSITY

Everyone must determine his or her own worries, friendships, priorities and responsibilities, and then commit to them. For me, that means living each day as if I have no tomorrow, and never forgetting I'm part of the natural world surrounding me.

The author's father, Ervin Perry Hamilton, shown here on his wedding day in 1936, could be a difficult, impatient parent. Judy believes time heals wounds and softens pain, but they never disappear. Even so, from the vantage point of time, she now more easily sees her father's strengths, shortcomings and good intentions.

Whether I'm outside or gazing from my window, I always look for animals, large and small. I watch the trees and their leaves, and I watch the clouds and listen to the wind. I make room for these things in my everyday life, and realize every living creature adapts as it encounters threats and challenges.

I watch when and how hornets build their nests. If they build high in the tree, I assume the winter that follows will be mild. If they build close to the ground, I expect lots of deep snow and numbing winds. When I look at trees, I note whether their limbs hang toward the ground. If they do, I know water shouldn't be far below the surface. But if their limbs grow straight toward the sun, I know water is nowhere near the surface. I also pay attention to the soft maple's leaves. Just before a rain, these trees turn their leaves upward, or as some say, inside out.

If you're hunting and a lightning storm approaches, your obvious priority is to seek shelter. There's no arguing with such a powerful force! But if a storm is upon you before you realize your predicament, and you feel the hair on your neck, arms or head rising, hit the ground. This is lightning's way of announcing its impending arrival!

On a less-hazardous front, always watch out for a fuzzy-looking plant we call itch weed. When it contacts your skin, it causes unbelievable burning and itching. Find the nearest water, collect some mud and smear it where you itch. Sure, you'll stop itching in a few hours anyway, but why suffer until then?

STRICT UPBRINGING

In much the same way, we learn to cope with our own internal storms and hazards. I keep supportive thoughts and wishful remedies in mind when contemplating my own life, but I do my best to avoid self-pity. No one who leads an easy life ever amounts to much. That much is sure. So when I discuss hardships I've experienced, I'm not seeking pity or empathy. I share my stories to pass along lessons I've learned firsthand, and possibly even inspire some hope.

Herman thinks I had a rough childhood, and that it must have been terrible to not have indoor plumbing until I was in eighth grade. We always heated our home with wood, never gas or oil. I didn't think about it. It was just our life. The trees were there, so why not use them?

Father could be a difficult person, but as Herman says, he worked hard and did his best. Herman views my dad this way:

"He gave Judy stern guidance, and sheltered her while she was growing up. But no matter how harsh he was, I still admire him. He was his own man. I could not have survived as his son, but Judy turned out to be an extraordinary person. Although I admire Ervin, I believe he never knew or recognized the beautiful person within his daughter. Judy was his only child. If he had three sons, none would have

Judy and Herman Kovar drive many miles each year to visit schools, civic groups and deer seminars. Wherever she goes, Judy reaches out to children and their parents. Her message to parents is to be responsible, pay attention to your children, and realize parenting is a never-ending responsibility.

been better than his lone daughter. I always tell Judy she was raised like a boy and punished for being a girl. I am proud of her heritage and her feelings for others. This must have come from her mother's side, and the Indian spirits that made her a survivor. I hope Judy's children will be proud of their blood and the importance of their heritage."

I read Herman's words and, from the vantage point of time, I now more easily see Father's strengths, shortcomings and good intentions. As the years separate us from events, all things change, often for the better. Time heals wounds and softens pain, but some pains never vanish. Either way, life goes on, and new pains replace or merge with old ones. Maybe we just become better at bearing our loads. I try to learn and grow from them all, and live life to its fullest. The only other choice is to let pain destroy you.

As rough as my childhood might sound, I don't envy today's children and the world they face. Many of these wonderful young people are exposed often to drugs, alcohol, street dangers, criminal activity and other negative influences. And they often must cope on their own. My father might have been harsh, but he was there and I knew where he stood. It's vital that all of us lend guidance and a kind heart to children, because they need help to be strong.

The sad reality is that we can't take the place of their parents, even when asked by the sweetest children we meet. Still, we must try to do our part. By driving many miles each year to visit schools, civic groups and deer seminars, I try to tattoo a positive image on their minds. My message to parents is to be responsible adults, pay attention to your children, and realize parenting is a never-ending responsibility. Children benefit greatly by hearing positive messages from other adults, because it makes them feel part of a community. When parents reinforce those adults' wise words and refer to them when using their own real-life examples to teach valuable lessons, maybe, just maybe, those lessons will sink in.

PROBLEMS, LARGE AND SMALL

Although our childhoods and personal lives aren't as charmed and sweetly seasoned as we would likely prefer, I must say the world of hunting isn't always kind, either. Especially for women.

From the time Herman got me into bowhunting, I encountered problems, large and small. Some came from simple jealousies, some from insecurities, and some from hostilities I'll never understand. In fact, my first bad bowhunting experience happened on my father's property. No one expects to get harassed on her father's land, but I'm proof it can happen.

One evening, two men met me at Father's property line and claimed that the permanent stand Dad and I had built was community property. That is, whoever occupied it first got to hunt there. One of them even made a veiled threat filled with curses: I could be mistaken for a deer and get shot in the back, and nobody would ever know who did it.

That evening I visited my parents and told Father about the encounter, and he handled it in his usual fashion: The next morning, we drove the tractor back to the site and he chain-sawed that huge 80-year-old tree to the ground!

Father reasoned that if I couldn't hunt there and feel safe, then nobody could hunt there. To retaliate, those two "sportsmen" regularly trespassed into Father's cornfield, picked his corn, and piled it on their side of the road near a pond to bait the deer, a practice that's also illegal in Illinois.

These days, I mostly hunt the little 120-acre farm that Herman and I own. I like to think it's our little slice of paradise, but I know some people will never respect another's property. Such disregard is not unique to my region, my state or anywhere in North America. As I travel to do sports shows and give deer seminars, I hear many sad stories from hunters disrespected by their fellow hunters.

The author hears many sad stories from hunters who have been disrespected by their fellow hunters. We disgrace our ancestors with such acts. All of us have free will. We can instill new values, stop the cycle of mistakes, and bring pride to our ancestors' names.

I wish time and experience improved such conduct, but I find little proof new generations strive to do so. We disgrace our ancestors with such acts, even if they're the ones who started their families down the wrong path. All of us have free will, and so we can instill new values, stop the cycle of mistakes, and bring pride to our ancestors' names.

WOMEN REMAIN POORLY EQUIPPED

On a lighter, but still serious note, I've resigned myself to a different problem—one shared and endured by nearly every female bowhunter I know: the clothing and equipment just aren't designed for us.

From the time I started trapping, I realized most clothes suited for the outdoors are designed for men. And I guess this problem started even earlier for me. I remember Mother putting me into boy's clothing for school and going to town. I hated it then and I hate it now.

Unfortunately, women often have little choice but to make men's clothing work for them, even though we often endanger ourselves in the process. I can't count how many times I've gotten stuck straddling a fence because the crotch of my pants restricted my movements. Ditto for waders. They're too big and too long, and have almost gotten me drowned.

Similar problems occur with coats and jackets. During a memorable bowhunt in a state park, I couldn't fully draw my bow because the coat's material bunched up on my shoulders. No matter what I tried, it kept binding on me as I neared full draw. I had to act fast. Every time the buck walked behind a tree, I removed another article of clothing. Then, with the coveralls hanging below my knees and my upper body sporting only insulated underwear, I finally pulled the bow to full draw. And then let down. By then the buck was too far away for a shot I felt comfortable taking.

That story might sound funny now, but I saw nothing to laugh about at the time as the buck walked into bow range and right back out while I stripped off clothing.

I choose boots carefully, but it's not easy. I've worn too many boots that never fit well, which blistered my feet and froze my toes even with two pairs of socks.

We need to realize that cold weather affects women more quickly than it does men. A woman's blood vessels are closer to the skin's surface, where they're more easily chilled.

Women often ask how I keep from freezing while bowhunting in cold weather. They say it's nearly impossible to stay warm, quiet and still on cold days. Their husbands and boyfriends are often no help. Physiologically, men are better equipped to handle cold temperatures and think women just need to "buck up" and deal with it.

Proper fitting clothing and footwear helps so much, and I encourage their purchase whenever possible. But even with the best boots and garments money can buy, you're wise to carry small heat packs in your pockets, under your toes, atop your kidneys and anywhere else you can slide or stick them! Some packets are air-activated, and others can be boiled and reused after reactivating them with a metal clicker.

Even with the best boots and garments money can buy, you're wise to carry small heat packs in your pockets, under your toes, atop your kidneys and anywhere else you can slide or stick them!

It pays to buy good clothing and learn how best to layer it for maximum performance, even if you stock up on heat packs. I especially love wearing wool in cold weather. Yes, it's expensive, but think how much money you've already wasted on clothing that doesn't fit or keep you warm! I've had a special wool vest made for me, and I stipulated that it have zippered pockets over each breast for my heat packs. This extra heat helps keep me warm, and if it's really cold I also put a larger heat pack over my lower back.

As you study clothing, look for garments using Polar fleece, Thinsulate, Thermax, Gore-Tex, Windstopper and other "miracle" materials. Believe me, technology has provided many wonderful benefits when it comes to outdoor clothing and footwear. We don't have to be miserably cold anymore!

Gloves are a problem because most are made for men's larger hands and longer fingers. I've often solved this problem by buying children's gloves, but you might have to do some customizing because they don't always come in camo colors. Also, I slip heat packs into the palms of gloves or mittens to keep my hands warm.

Clothing designs, although they've improved in variety and function, remain a challenge. You can't just run down to the nearest store and find a wide variety of women's hunting clothes. And be warned: If you want to wear camo coveralls, realize they present real problems in common situations. Whenever I zip them up, things

Although the author took many fine whitetails with her Martin Dynabow during the late 1980s and early 1990s, she is grateful that women today have far more options in hunting bows. She prefers a lightweight bow that can be adjusted up to 60 pounds.

go smoothly until the zipper reaches my bust line. I then must tuck, poke, and suck in to finish zipping. Women need coveralls with more room in the chest, but without a corresponding width increase in the shoulders or length increases in the arms and legs!

Yes, women bowhunters experience difficulties when making do with men's clothing. One option is taking those coveralls to a seamstress to get them professionally altered, but that's expensive. A better option is to plan ahead and research the large mail-order catalogs. Realize manufacturers are listening to women, but finding what you need is seldom going to be fast or convenient. As one manufacturer told me, there still just aren't enough female hunters to make women's hunting clothes a profitable market.

BOWS AND ARROWS

Obviously, most women struggle to hold and draw many bows designed for men. We've seen some real advances in bows and arrows to accommodate women, but again, you must do some homework and plan your purchases. A bow's actual weight, as well as its cams, draw weight and speed, all must be considered when a woman begins bowhunting.

Few women have the strength to handle 70-pound draw weights. I've also noticed when I hold my bow in a ground blind—where it's seldom possible to keep it hanging at the ready—my arms tire quickly. The solution is a lighter bow, one that weighs three to four pounds, but can be adjusted to reach a 60-pound draw weight.

I also advise women, as well as middle-aged and older men, to stay away from radical cams. Some of these cams are difficult to "break over" when drawing the bow, which puts undue strain on your shoulders. If you struggle to pull your bow easily and pain-free in practice, you'll never get to full draw once your muscles are subjected to autumn winds and frosty temperatures. I stick with a fairly round cam on my bows, and work with archery experts to ensure I'm choosing the best option.

Women and archery instructors should also understand that a woman's shooting stance must be tweaked to fit her physique. Granted, there is a proper way to stand and shoot, but a fully endowed woman must find a stance that protects her from the string's release. One answer is a chest protector, and these days Neet Archery offers camo versions that not only help women but also hold down bulky clothing in cold weather. Even so, my ancestors didn't use chest protectors, and I think many women are better off in the long run to adjust their stance. Turn your feet and body so that when you break the bow over and anchor, the bowstring lies gently on the side of your left breast, assuming you're shooting right-handed. Experiment until you find what works, making sure nothing comes between the drawn bowstring and the rear of your bow.

Arrows also require attention because most women don't pull draw weights that shoot heavy arrows very well. When we go with lighter arrows, we gain some speed to flatten our shooting trajectories. When Easton first sent me a dozen carbon arrows to shoot, Herman and I were doubtful they'd perform well with my 60-pound draw weight. We soon changed our minds when we found that we could use the same sight pin to shoot out to 30 yards.

I'm not writing an advertisement for carbon arrows, but they do remove some guesswork from judging distances. This leaves one less frustration for beginners to experience. Anytime you can remove doubts, you decrease stress and increase enjoyment.

Another of my initial fears with carbon shafts was how they would handle broadheads. I don't shoot the poundage or heavy arrow shafts that handle heavy, oversized broadheads. However, it's also possible to choose broadheads that are too small. For years I always shot heavy, fixed-blade broadheads and was impressed with their performance. When I switched to carbon arrows, I found they did not accommodate large broadheads and carry them truly through the air. Herman was shooting replaceable-blade broadheads, so I switched to them.

Of course, good equipment doesn't solve every problem or challenge. Many remain up to us. One attribute I'm proud to see in most female bowhunters is their willingness to pass up long shots.

My maximum shooting distance on game animals is 25 yards. I'm not confident or comfortable with shots longer than that. I never compare myself to Herman in my shooting style or success. I found what was right for me and stuck with it. Granted, sometimes that requires willpower, but it's an important goal to maintain.

Some women who learn about archery by "shooting paper" struggle making the transition from target archery to bowhunting. No matter how you develop your archery interest, realize everything changes once you're in the woods and an animal is approaching. Shooting at paper will always be far different from shooting at an animal, and the woods will never offer a controlled environment.

No matter how you develop your archery interest, realize everything changes once you're in the woods and an animal is approaching. Shooting at paper will always be far different from shooting at an animal.

The next best step is a 3-D outdoor range, which can simulate hunting situations. Wind can influence your arrow's flight and twigs can deflect your best shot, but unlike a living whitetail, a 3-D deer target won't jump the string and duck beneath your streaking arrow.

The only way to build your confidence is to be out in the woods as much as possible. The more you're out there, the more likely you'll feel at ease when animals approach. Herman even admits that the first few times he goes out each autumn, he gets the shakes when he sees deer. Only by being out there with the animals can you cure "Buck-a-Ger," which is what Mother called getting the shakes. She said it's the only disease that doesn't cause high temperatures, but can be cured by an arrow drawing blood.

To recap, bowhunters must feel comfortable and confident with their bow and equipment, they must have clothes that can keep them in the woods and able to draw their bow, and they must have the confidence to hit their quarry squarely and kill it cleanly. When you can meet those three requirements—whether you're a man, woman or youngster—you'll enjoy consistent bowhunting success.

Bowhunters must feel comfortable and confident with their bow and equipment, they must have clothes that can keep them in the woods and able to draw their bow, and they must have the confidence to hit their quarry squarely and kill it cleanly.

Compared to those factors, choosing between tree stands and ground blinds is a secondary matter! I enjoy bowhunting from the ground, and encourage other women to try it. I feel I'm well prepared for this approach. I'm the one who disinfects, scrubs floors, wears perfume, applies make-up and washes clothes. Such habits give me a different perspective on bowhunting than most men, which leaves me better prepared to use scents and "make-up" in the field.

I watch the wind and my scent more than Herman does. I use deer urine and rut scents as if they were perfume, and treat them as such. I apply them carefully when preparing to sit. Herman does not. Again, I see things differently and hunt accordingly.

DEALING WITH OTHER ILL WINDS

I only wish that rumors, greed and jealousies were as easily addressed as finding the right boots, clothing, bows and arrows. I don't know what it is, but as a group, hunters are often sickeningly competitive and jealous, gossiping without shame when someone else tastes consistent success. And I say without doubt that they gossip even more if the successful hunter is female.

About the time I had two white-tailed bucks in the Pope & Young record book, and a third waiting to be scored and entered, I started hearing remarks that no woman could bow-kill two or three whitetails of that caliber. When Herman and I went to the archery range to practice, guys often stood behind us to size me up and judge my ability. Some stared through the hallway glass and whispered among themselves.

I felt hurt. I was proud of what I had accomplished, yet here were grown men trying to find fault and question my skills and accomplishments. Herman would pull me aside, tell me to pay no attention, remind me that I knew the truth, and that I had experienced worse pain. He reminded me I had nothing to prove to anyone.

Neither the jealousy of some hunters nor the hatred of animal-rights activists deter the author from enjoying archery and bowhunting, and sharing her experiences through articles and public presentations.

To this day I still heed his words, but it's not easy. When my third record-book buck was verified, the comments worsened, my self-esteem took a beating, and inner conflicts returned. I felt like hanging my head instead of holding it up proudly. And then, as if by evil design, a second campaign of hate arose against me, orchestrated by a Connecticut group called The Friends of Animals.

I had been writing for The Trapper & Predator Caller, Turkey Caller and L.A.N.D. magazines, and the animal-rights crowd wanted me silenced. They decided it was wrong for me to trap and bowhunt.

I received late-night phone calls and mass-mailed hate letters. The phone calls were always the same: "Do you know what you are? You are a murderer! Slime! You prey on helpless animals. What you do to them shall be done to you."

This torment included UPS packages that contained decaying animal parts and jars of clotted blood. I felt sorry for the UPS driver because he was afraid to make deliveries. He felt even worse when I told him what was inside the boxes he brought me.

Eventually, I considered giving up my work and never writing another article. I also considered never teaching another trapping class, or even bowhunting another deer. Then I thought of my grandfather and mother. I would not let someone else decide what was right for me, whether they hunted or opposed hunting. I had never met the animal-rights activists, and they certainly didn't know me. They had never walked in my shoes, felt my feelings, or listened to my loved ones. Grandfather wouldn't have been intimidated by those cowards, so neither would I. If anything, I would continue everything I was doing just to torment them.

Their challenges reminded me of my chosen mission. I had been following the path Grey Wolf had predicted for a long time already, and I had too much blood, pride and joy invested in that path and my life's circle. Hadn't Grandfather foreseen many battles and skirmishes along the way for me? My life's journey had survived much more difficult, heart-rending tests, and I decided I would not dishonor my ancestors by letting my least worthy challengers push me from my chosen path. ■

13

SCRAPES AND MOCK SCRAPES

I've played around with scrapes and different deer urines for years. I guess it goes back to my interest in trapping and my ancestors. My people were experts at scents, and using the animals' odors to play one critter against the other.

My interest in scents increased markedly a few years ago when I went two years without tagging a whitetail. I realized I needed to try some new ideas, so I sought help from Lee Rotzien at Lee's Pure Deer Urine in Michigan. Lee sent a bottle of fawn urine and a small set of rattling antlers. Talk about small! Those antlers might have measured three inches high from the base! Lee said, "If you can't find the big ones, start with the little ones." I assumed the package was just a joke.

The next few weeks I worked on a big buck whose antler spread was about 22 to 23 inches. I was using doe and buck urines by the bottles. One morning while heading out the door in the dark, I grabbed the wrong bottle of deer lure. When I reached the field I planned to watch, I pulled out the bottle and noticed it was Lee's bottle of fawn urine. Dawn was breaking, and I didn't have time to run home for the right bottle, so I opened the bottle of fawn urine and poured at least half of it into a huge scrape.

The author has always made deer scents part of her bowhunts, using them to doctor scrapes, lay scent trails and cover human odors. In November 2002, Judy arrowed this huge whitetail with help from Buck Stop scents. The 11-pointer weighed 330 pounds undressed, and its 146 net score gave Judy her seventh entry into the Pope & Young Club's record book.

I set up nearby and waited, but my heart wasn't in it. How could I have made such a mistake? This was no time to mess up on this buck. He regularly had three to four does with him, and he couldn't care less about food or fawns.

The day passed quietly and I went home at dark, disgusted with myself. When I arose the next morning I grabbed the right bottle of urine and headed back.

When I entered the field, the area around me looked like a battlefield. The trees and sumacs were ripped up, and limbs were strewn everywhere. The air reeked of buck urine. In the thin light, I could also see smaller scrapes had been opened around the dominant one. What had infuriated this buck? I decided the only thing different from my previous visits was that bottle of fawn urine.

Legitimate scrapes always have an overhanging branch. If you find a field that's ringed with scrapes, pay no attention to those without a limb overhead. Limb-free scrapes are made by immature bucks that are all charged up but don't have a clue what they're doing.

I called Lee and told him if he sent that first bottle of fawn urine as a joke, then please tell the joke again! Three days later I was again pouring fawn urine into that big scrape. And again, the buck went on a destructive rampage! This time, though, I was nearby when he thrashed the brush and dashed from one end of the valley to the other, saliva dripping from his mouth.

That evening I called Lee to discuss the situation. What would a mature buck do if it believed a baby buck was messing with his scrape? I hadn't thought about it, but maybe I had been challenging that buck's dominance, slapping him in the face by pouring fawn urine into his primary scrape. I think that flipped his switch. He wanted to drub that little buck, re-mark his territory and defend it. In the process, he was being less cautious and leaving himself vulnerable.

OPENING A WINDOW

The more I thought about it, the more convinced I became that fawn urine had inadvertently opened a new window into scrapes and mock scrapes. I also started looking for more ways to use fawn urine. I began to lightly spray it onto my pant legs. After all, no matter how carefully I entered and left my hunting areas, I always left behind human scent by brushing against branches, sticks, brush and tall grass above my rubber boots. Now I leave behind fawn scent instead.

The ploy seems to work. When that grandma doe clears the way for all others, she's less likely to spook when crossing my path. Because she smells more fawn than human scents, no alarm bells go off. Instead, she often tries to find the new kid on the block.

I notice that bucks have similar reactions. They cut across the trail and seem more curious than alarmed.

Yes, fawn urine has a true purpose in the deer woods. I now use it as a cover scent in early fall, October and into November when I'm having trouble getting near a buck with too many does. I figure that when bowhunters realize its universal application, fawn urine will find a permanent place in their fanny packs.

Every edge helps when does far outnumber bucks, and you see far fewer rubs and scrapes. In these situations, most bucks are too busy to advertise. True, you'll see situations where a hayfield or soybean field is ringed with scrapes, but some of them won't have an overhanging branch. Those scrapes are usually made by immature bucks that can't get near a harem. Their hormones run hot and they think they know what to do about it, but they can't find a willing partner anywhere! Instead, these lovelorn boys take out their aggressions in the dirt, and on brush and saplings.

If you're not interested in a trophy buck, these youngsters are easily bow-killed. A mock scrape and a little hot doe urine usually gets these starry-eyed bucks

When creating a mock scrape, pick a site near a deer trail or travel corridor. Also check for nearby rubs and, if you find one, count the gouges from the buck's tines. The distance between brow-tine gouges gives you an idea of its antler spread.

into bow range. You can't bowhunt every scrape they make, so you'll do better making a mock scrape to entice them onto your playground.

Everything is much different when dealing with trophy whitetails. They don't bother with scrapes that lack an overhanging branch. Bucks use these limbs for scent-marking and monitoring the presence of other bucks in the area.

That branch is a key to your success.

CANCELING SCRAPES

When you encounter a situation in which a buck isn't checking the scrapes regularly, try canceling a scrape of his and making a mock scrape. You want him to think you're the new buck in town, and you're there to court his ladies.

The first step in canceling a buck's scrape is to break off every overhanging branch the buck might be scent-marking. Now, take those branches out of the area and dump them. If you hang old scent branches above your new mock scrape, you'll lose the antagonistic element of being the new buck. You want the buck you're hunting to think that he is being disrespected by an intruder.

Next, cover the existing scrape with dirt and leaves to make it look like the rest of the woods. You want it to lose all of its eye and scent appeal. After canceling the scrape, leave a light scent trail from there to your mock scrape.

After preparing a mock scrape or doctoring an existing scrape, hang a tarsal gland from the overhanging branch. Scent from a tarsal gland communicates disrespect to other bucks using the scrape.

To create your mock scrape, start by choosing a site along a deer trail or travel corridor, and be sure it's on fairly level ground. Also, look around for signs of the buck's presence. When you find a rub, always count indentations from its tines, and check the amount of damage to surrounding brush and the side of the tree the rub is on. Such signs tell you what direction the whitetail is traveling. Measure the distance between the brow-tine marks on the rubs. This gives you an idea of the buck's antler spread. Look for patterns of rubs that indicate the buck is defending an area or marking time there, such as rub lines or staging areas.

When you pick the actual scrape site, make sure it includes an overhanging branch. Next, clear the ground and the upper layers of dirt. That buck knows every inch of his woods, and he definitely notices freshly exposed, well-worked soil.

I know from my years of trapping that the dirt at the set is very important. A fox paws and digs without hesitation when I mix dirt from a chicken house with the dirt at a trap site. With mock scrapes, the principle is similar, but we don't necessarily care if the buck paws the scrape. We just want him to stay there long enough for us to aim and unleash our arrow.

If a buck smells fresh dirt and scent, and it finds tracks, droppings and a new rub nearby, it starts thinking another buck is infringing on its turf. When a mature buck decides to restore order in the woods' hierarchy, it makes itself more vulnerable.

However, I've also tried moving dirt from one authentic scrape to another, but this method seems to work best on young bucks. Some yearling bucks get their hackles up and turn aggressive when I've moved soiled dirt between scrapes. I never notice much difference when trying this tactic on older, dominant bucks.

OK, now that you've worked up the soil, it's time to hang a tarsal gland from the overhanging branch. That tarsal gland provides the other buck's scent and communicates disrespect. When hanging a tarsal gland over a mock scrape, keep an eye on it. I usually leave it for about a week, and then decide whether temperatures have been too warm and spoiled it, or if it's still good for a few more miles. In the latter case, I resoak it in deer urine or refreeze it. I've frozen glands for two years, and they still soak up urine and work as well as fresh ones.

The next step requires doe scent. During the early season, I go with regular doe urine, but then go to hot-doe lures as the rut approaches. Remove the scent bottle's cap and slide in an unscented absorbent cotton, such as a regular tampon. Now, put the cap back on and put it inside your pocket to warm it up. By the time you reach the scrape the urine will be warm, helping its odor carry farther. Once there, remove the cotton from the bottle and hang it on the overhanging branch. The advantage of using tampons is that they come with a string, so tying them to branches is easy.

As long as you keep that scented cotton hanging above the scrape, it will dispense urine into the dirt for you. Simply reapply scent to the cotton as needed to keep fresh scent dripping into the scrape. If you're lucky enough to hunt every day and don't want the buck to get used to the urine, untie the cotton and return it to the doe-urine bottle occasionally.

Some bowhunters make sets of three mock scrapes, arranging them in a triangular pattern around their tree stand or blind. When using various scents, drippers and scouting cameras, do so in increments so you can better judge what works and what doesn't before making further changes.

I prefer to change the doe urine every two to three days, hoping to make the buck think lots of new deer are in his area. You want to make him curious, give him reasons to keep investigating your mock scrape.

To ensure I can keep changing the scents in my mock scrapes, I keep several absorbent-cotton lure-holders in different bottles of doe urine. Whenever I hunt the scrape, I take out the holder and tie it into the overhanging branch. In two or three days I return, take that one down and hang a different urine, be it a fawn, plain doe, doe-in-heat, regular buck, buck-in-rut, dominant buck, etc. These changes pique the buck's curiosity. My intention is to cause him to lower his guard while defending his breeding rights.

TIPS AND TRICKS

After clearing the ground, and hanging the tarsal gland and urine-soaked cotton, I always sprinkle a few deer pellets into the scrape. Sometimes I even take an old deer hoof and put some tracks into the freshly tilled turf, too.

If you plan to bowhunt over your mock scrape the day you make it, be sure to wear latex or rubber gloves while you work. However, I usually work bare handed or wearing clean cotton gloves, because I prefer to wait at least two or three days before bowhunting a new mock scrape. Why the two- or three-day wait? When I trapped furbearers, I found it takes about that long for human scent to "burn off."

A white-tailed buck takes account of everything, so if it sees and smells fresh dirt, tracks, droppings, different odors and maybe a new rub or two, it starts believing there's an upstart punk of a buck hanging around that needs to be taught some respect. As the mature buck sets out to restore the pecking order, he exposes himself to danger. That jealous, protective instinct has allowed me to arrow almost all of my trophy bucks.

As you lay your trap, however, realize that mature buck won't tolerate mistakes. Keep your own odors to a minimum, stay downwind of the scrape, and make as little impact on the area as possible. That buck might be revved up from the rut, but he won't ignore your presence. If you don't take every precaution possible, all your other efforts will be wasted.

WISE USE

Many bowhunters remain leery of using whitetail urines, telling me they've had bad experiences with them. Don't be too quick to give up. First, buy from reputable companies, and make sure they supply urines from actual white-tailed deer. But realize, too, that you must take care of these scents. Don't leave them in direct sunlight or anywhere else that's hot. And don't count on them to cover your mistakes. If you're sloppy in the woods, and taint your hunting site with your own odors, no amount of doe or buck urine will make up for it.

Don't forget the boredom factor either. Deer quit responding if they smell the same scent day after day. Eventually, they shy away from certain odors, knowing some never produced action when they noticed them on previous visits. You can reduce the chances of boring them if you make better use of the deer themselves. Every time you shoot a whitetail, cut off its tarsal glands, store them in a plastic bag in your freezer, and reuse them later. Whenever Herman and I see a road-killed deer or arrow our own, we get out a pocket-knife and remove those tarsal glands, whether it's a buck or doe. By soaking the gland three days in buck urine, it takes on the desired odor.

When you're field-dressing a deer and notice its bladder is full, drain it into a glass bottle and freeze it. You don't need to buy everything prepackaged! Droppings are the easiest of all to collect and save. They can be found year-round, stored in bottles and frozen. In other words, never forsake the basics. Besides, it saves you lots of money!

I prefer to store deer urines in glass bottles. Why? Glass is impervious to odors. In comparison, plastic containers compromise a scent's odor. If you don't believe it, take a one-gallon plastic milk jug and store the milk in your refrigerator next to a freshly peeled onion. By morning your milk smells and tastes like onions! Granted, plastic is lighter to carry and doesn't break, but just carrying it can taint your deer lures.

If you leave the plastic jug inside your truck on the dashboard, the lure will pick up smoke, oil and human odors as it freezes, thaws and refreezes. Glass, meanwhile, doesn't allow foreign orders to invade it, but neither is it forgiving when contents inside it freeze. To avoid having freezing liquid break the glass with, always leave lots of extra room in the bottle, and freeze it inside a solid plastic bag, just to be safe.

In recent years, I've increasingly used scent-laden gels because of their ability to stay put and retain their odor in all kinds of weather. These products also save money and time when you're preparing and maintaining mock scrapes.

As with all other aspects of bowhunting, don't be afraid to experiment with scents and mock scrapes. Some people make sets of three mock scrapes, arranging them in a triangular pattern around their tree stand or blind. As you work with different scents, drippers and scouting cameras, do so in increments so you can better judge what works and what doesn't before making further changes. These are always fun, educational experiments, giving yet another reason to get into the woods whenever possible. ■

14

THE GREAT FLOOD

Herman had just gone through another spinal surgery around July 4, 1993, and I had been at his bedside all day, every day. I couldn't do much outside anyway. Rain had been falling for weeks, but I hadn't given it much thought because of Herman's condition.

Soon after I brought him home, a visit from a state policeman changed our lives forever. As the policeman drove down our driveway and past the beautiful apple trees flanking it, he started honking his horn. When I answered the door he didn't waste words: "Judy, this is it! The levee broke and an 11-foot wall of water is heading your way!"

My mind raced but it found no traction. All I knew for sure was that we had to get Herman out. After that, everything seemed equally important, and I wanted to take it all. This wasn't fair! Do we take clothes? No. We should take pictures. They can't be replaced. Still, I stood in the kitchen, frozen by indecision, as the policeman took Herman out. I wanted to take Grandmother's green crystal goblets, my quilts and my wedding dress. And we needed our bed, furniture, tools and … it was all too much to carry! Instead I snatched photos from the walls and plucked medicine bottles off the counter.

Suddenly, I heard the policeman yelling at me: "Come on! Now!"

I did as he instructed. Let's face it. You just don't start piling stuff into a state policemen's car. Our deer heads and some bows were already in the trailer because we had loaded it for an upcoming show, so they went with us.

Judy and Herman Kovar's life changed forever on July 18, 1993, when a massive flood destroyed their cherished home. This photo shows their well-kept house shortly before an 11-foot levee broke and floodwaters poured across the land.

As we drove down the lane to safety, I turned to take what would be my last look at our farm and home. All our countless hours of labor and love were within that house's walls. Tears streaked my cheeks and I tried to be strong, but I felt like dying.

The summer before the Great Flood, Judy and Herman paused for this photo with good friend Mel Johnson of Peoria, Illinois. (center). Bowhunters might recognize Mel as the man who arrowed the Pope & Young Club's record typical white-tailed buck in 1965—a record that was still standing more than 40 years later. When the flood receded, five months after inundating the Kovars' home, Mel was one of the first to arrive to help them put things back together.

Herman and I will never forget July 18, 1993, because part of our lives ended that day. Within minutes, nearly everything we owned was gone, including most of our clothes, our mounted turkey, animal pelts and hides, my Indian artifacts and tools, including Grandmother's bone needles and scrapers that I showed and explained to the schoolchildren. Whenever I see similar scenes on TV after hurricanes, tornadoes or tsunamis, my heart aches for those poor people. No one should have to go through such loss and heartache.

As we coped with our loss in the days that followed, all we could do was look ahead two weeks to the Volunteer State Deer Classic in Nashville, Tennessee. No matter who we consulted, we got the same answer: Floodwaters would occupy our home for the foreseeable future. Because we suddenly had nothing to keep us in Illinois, we left early for Nashville.

Upon arriving at the hotel, we received a Federal Express letter from the Easton Technical Products in Salt Lake City. Enclosed were a check and a heartfelt note from Mike Day, in which he told us to buy some clothes and take care of ourselves.During the show, we were overwhelmed by similar sentiments from everyone we met. Strangers approached to give us a hug or to offer donations. The days ran together, causing us to lose track of the date and weekday, but it seemed that no one at the event forgot about us. As the show finally neared its end, its owner and director, Glenn Helgeland of Target Communications, handed us an envelope. Within it were the hopes and prayers of all the show's exhibitors, along with generous donations.

FACING THE DISASTER

Finally, we had to return home and face the disaster. By then the Great Flood of 1993—when the Mississippi and Illinois rivers overflowed and overwhelmed everything in their paths for hundreds of miles—was already being forgotten, except by those who had been caught in its path. We lived from place to place for weeks, accepting help from many and eating meals from the Red Cross's food wagon. For medical attention we visited disaster-relief shelters, and if they couldn't help, we rode a helicopter to the hospital.

I still relive those painful days and weeks daily. No one should have to decide between family heirlooms, clothes, pictures and other valuables as an unseen wall of water rushes toward them. Unless you've lived through such disasters, it's impossible to understand how fast water can rise, or know what an 11-foot wall of water will do to property and human life long after its fury ends and the floodwaters recede.

I'm sometimes baffled when people ask why we were living in a floodplain. If you're anywhere near a large river or stream, you're usually living in a floodplain. In our case, we lived seven miles downstream from where the levee broke. We had believed the Army Corps of Engineers spokesmen, who had long assured us such floods would never happen. We were told the levees were strong and that we would be safe. We had no reason to doubt them.

Then again, the flood of 1993 was called a 500-year flood. I have to smile at the irony. How many people were around in 1493 to record the devastation of such floods in America's midsection? When this event struck that summer, floodwaters from the Mississippi and Illinois rivers washed across lands that had never been touched in modern times by river waters. In our case, our home, farm and almost everything we owned was covered with 15 feet of water for 109 days, from July 18 through November 4, and it took most of November before the water left the farm for good.

There's no arguing with a flood. With waters nearly covering their home, all Judy and Herman could do was wait for the flood to recede. At this point, they knew they would be able to salvage little from their home.

During those dreadful waterlogged months, when nothing was certain, people asked why we weren't doing things for ourselves. Some of them called us freeloaders for eating at the Red Cross or accepting towels and medical attention. One woman even told me I should be thankful for losing our home, property and belongings. She said: "Feel blessed, young lady, because God has given you what you deserve!"

Herman ignored her, but I couldn't suffer such nonsense! I told her what I thought of her meanness, and she left in a huff. Years later, people asked if we were back in the house or working the farm. Little did they realize, we never returned.

As the floodwaters gradually receded during the late summer and throughout autumn 1993, the Kovars' home deteriorated and began breaking apart. All they could do was conduct rescue missions for small animals trapped atop roofs and other structures.

What house did they have in mind? The den from our home was ripped away and never found. Our roof ended up on the first floor and in the basement. Our bedroom broke away from the main part of the building and collapsed. One of the walls was

About twelve feet of water still covered the Kovars' home and buildings in November 1993, four months after the flood first hit. Not until this photo was taken in late December 1993 would the Kovars again see ground in their yard. When they returned to salvage their belongings, they found nearly everything had disappeared with the water.

found three miles away. No, we didn't return home one day, call the newspaper to resume deliveries, and go about our daily routines.

We never did find our archery shop; not a wall, nor the roof, or anything. The floodwaters did things we never knew possible. We found some pennies that had been reduced to a solid lump, as if heated with a blowtorch. The water ate and destroyed nearly everything it touched, whether it was metal, cloth, wood paneling or drywall. The only thing left on our home's interior walls and ceiling were bare studs and roof trusses. All the paneling and drywall fell to the floor or washed into the basement.

Herman and I learned one never fully recovers from natural disasters. The government takes its time drafting settlement checks, insurance companies send their checks to the bank to pay the mortgage, and the bank isn't quick to make loans because floods often strip you of work and collateral. People think that once the water retreats, life instantly returns to normal. If only that were true. I often answered such questions by showing people recent photos of our home and property, and they gasped in horror and disbelief.

As the weeks turned into months, we eventually realized we would never return to our farm. The federal government forbade us from rebuilding there unless we elevated the house 19 feet into the air, four feet above where the water stopped rising on our property.

Believe me, sadness, stress and frustration don't float away with your belongings. They remain with you, stalwart as the mold and water stains that cling and discolor everything the water touched.

FOUR-LEGGED FLOOD VICTIMS

The flood's devastation wasn't limited to people, of course. Animals, wild and domestic, suffered, too. A few days after the levee broke, our local game warden, Gene Stumpf, loaded Herman and me into his boat and took us back to the farm. Among other things, I was worried about a den of red foxes and a couple of raccoons that had been hanging around our place, and I had heard reports of a baby fox floating atop a big round hay bale near the house. We loaded sacks and rope into Gene's boat and set off.

As we neared our farm, my heart sank. All we could see of our home's roof was its vent-turbines! Meanwhile, a roof floated by, and sitting atop it were squirrels, a rabbit and rats. We never located the stranded fox.

Gene maneuvered the boat close to the roof and then stepped onto it. I feared for his safety, but he quickly netted the rabbit and I put it in the burlap sack. The squirrel proved more difficult and ran laps around Gene, but we managed to get him. Such sights were routine in the days and weeks after the flood, and those animals had no idea what had happened to their world. Maybe it's easier that way. I don't know. Meanwhile, dead hogs, cattle and wildlife floated by. That wall of water had been too much for them.

When the radio reported a fawn trapped on a high part of the levee, we went to help. The young fawn looked pathetic. Floodwaters were up to its belly, and it had no dry place to lie down. It was so tired it laid its head on floating brush as it drifted by. The fawn obviously could not survive long, but every time our boat approached it would bleat and move toward deeper, swifter water. We waited a couple of days, and then tried a joint rescue effort. We couldn't use a tranquilizer, fearing the fawn would drown before we could reach it. We finally managed to rescue it, and we released it on high ground.

Gene burned up one 140-hp boat engine trying to save animals, and ferrying people to and from their farms and homes. As we talked with him during those rescue missions, he filled us in on what he saw in the hours after the flooding started. He was in a helicopter when the levee broke, and he watched the bigger whitetails flee the bottoms as water thundered through. The fawns didn't make it. In an instant, the Illinois River went from three-quarters of a mile wide to six or seven miles wide. Only the stronger, faster, larger animals reached safety. Animals like squirrels and raccoons climbed trees to ride out the torrents, but the rest had to rely on their ability to flee to higher ground. Animals that couldn't run fast or climb trees were swept away as if they were driftwood.

Only the stronger, faster, larger animals reached safety. Squirrels and raccoons climbed trees to ride out the torrents, but the rest had to rely on their ability to flee to higher ground. Animals that couldn't run fast or climb trees were swept away as if they were driftwood.

Adding to the terrible conditions were the farm crops, all of which were destroyed at incredible financial loss to farmers. The beans had been loaded with pods, the wheat was ready to harvest, and the corn was tasseling and carrying small ears. Within a few days, all that potential food separated from the plants and rose to the surface. All that mixed with other debris and began to rot, and the stench became overwhelming.

As I saw the bodies of small whitetails floating by, my heart cried. Those stranded in isolated pockets had little food to survive. The once food-rich bottoms remained underwater for weeks, and when animals returned looking for food, they found none and retreated to higher ground. With the waterline at 18 to 19 feet for weeks in the bottomlands, all browse was destroyed. The animals had no Red Cross workers and volunteers to direct them to food and shelter. Many died on nearby roads and highways as they searched far and wide for their next meal. They knew their home turf and yearned for it, but like us, they could only move to high ground and wait.

During that time, I picked up two dead fawns and asked a taxidermist to preserve them as mounts so that I could take them to my school presentations. I wanted children to know the look and feel of a fawn. I wanted to help them understand what is lost to nature's indifferent perils. I wanted children to feel the hurt, knowing these creatures and thousands like them didn't survive the flood's violent, muddy waters. One cannot learn everything by reading. Sometimes it takes a hands-on approach.

In September 1993, we finally rented a four-room house but, of course, it wasn't our home. Plus, reminders of the flood's impact remained everywhere. Herman often strapped on his pistol as if he were Sheriff Matt Dillon on Gunsmoke, and went into the basement to kill snakes that were seeking refuge there. Yeah, snakes were living in our basement. And much like ants at a picnic, for every snake Herman shot, it seemed two arrived for the funeral. They sure didn't give up easily.

RESOLUTE FRIENDS

Life was never easy in the flood's aftermath, but with 12 feet of water still covering our farm and house in early November 1993, we couldn't believe the continued support of our archery family. The donations kept showing up at least weekly, and they included pots, pans, utensils, linens, pillows, towels and other housewares, along with offers of new bows, knives, clothing, fletching and broadheads. Archers and bowhunters have so much capacity for goodness!

Our family of archery friends kept Herman and me together with their frequent calls. They reminded us often that they were only a phone call away, ready to travel long distances to help us clean up and rebuild.

Unfortunately, we came to hate the government, insurance companies, empty promises and red tape. We battled relentlessly over the farm's value, frustrated with a process that fostered insults, disrespect and confrontations. I often recalled Grey Wolf's comment that governmental papers paper blow in the wind like the spirits of dead warriors. He said such papers lie; the government writes what it wants, and then the papers get torn up and scattered as if they never existed.

The floodwaters didn't recede completely until nearly December. Soon after, Mel Johnson of Peoria, Illinois, was one of the first "outsiders" to show up. Mel's name might be familiar to many of you as the bowhunter who arrowed the Pope & Young Club's record typical white-tailed buck back in 1965—a record that still stands, more than 40 years later.

We crawled into our home through the roof, which now lay on the first floor. With Mel's help, we searched for our possessions, but almost everything had vanished in the flood. Mel salvaged plates and two of my grandmothers' green crystal goblets. We also found a few broken arrow artifacts and shattered picture frames. Everything bore scars, and each item brought more tears. All that destruction resembled our own lives and dreams.

I wiped away the tears and looked at the clouds drifting across the blue sky. I then sang a Northern Cheyenne death chant. That's what I felt like: a defeated warrior awaiting death. ■

15

DECOYING FOR THE GROUND POUNDER

I've enjoyed much excitement and success with decoys over the years. Not only are they fun to use, they're also a great aid for ground-pounders like me who know the challenges of drawing a bow undetected when you're at eye level with whitetails.

Talk about excitement! Once I watched a smaller buck, maybe a 4- or 6-pointer, sneak behind my decoy, wanting to come in, but never losing its caution. Maybe he had gotten his butt kicked before under similar circumstances. But I had that decoy smelling so good, the little buck couldn't resist coming in closer.

Decoys are practical hunting aids that generate lots of fun for bowhunters. Not only do they lure aggressive bucks into bow range, they hold the buck's undivided attention. This allows bowhunters to more easily come to full draw without being detected.

I've also had wide megabucks attack the decoy as it stood in a field, minding its own business. I've had smaller bucks try to mount the decoy. And I even saw two small bucks push and fight each other for the chance to court my decoy.

On at least a couple of occasions, however, the excitement didn't involve deer. I once watched a young red fox walk up and sit in front of my decoy, staring at it in wonder. I could almost read his fuzzy face: "Why don't you move? Are you sick? Something about you just isn't right!" Finally, after 10 minutes, the fox got up, walked over to the decoy, lifted his leg and urinated on the decoy's leg. I laughed out loud.

The author shot this 8-point trophy in November 1997 from her ground blind after calling and decoying it into range. Its net score of 128-3/8 earned Judy her sixth entry into the Pope & Young Club's record book.

I wasn't laughing during another decoy-aided hunt, however. I had my decoy out and was set up for the evening's hunt when three dogs ran from the woods an hour before dark. One of them, a big shepherd, ran at my doe decoy, grabbed it by the throat and took it down. The other two dogs joined in the attack. As I yelled and burst from my hiding place in the underbrush, the shepherd charged me! I raised the bow and yelled again, but to no avail.

The dog was less than 10 yards away and preparing to leap at me when I released the bow-string and put him down. Shaking, I returned to my vehicle and hurriedly drove home. Herman said the dogs were looking for deer when they attacked the decoy, and the doe urine on my clothing could have caused the attack.

This incident could have turned into a horrible accident. I hated to shoot that dog, but it wore no collar and its ribs were showing. Sometimes people move and leave their pets behind. We never learned if those dogs belonged to anyone.

The author shot this 140-inch 8-pointer in November 1993, notching her fifth entry in the Pope & Young Club's record book. Note that she likes using a single antler on her decoy. Bucks usually approach more quickly and confidently if they sense weakness in a rival. A one-antlered buck is at a real disadvantage.

Although decoys tend to work best during the rut, they can also work at other times during the archery season. Judy shot this impressive 8-pointer on January 8, 2004, while using a decoy.

AN AGE-OLD TACTIC

Decoying, the use of an animal facsimile to attract others of its kind, is as old as my ancestors. My forebears often wore deer hides and antlers to disguise themselves and decoy deer, and they wore wolf skins or buffalo hides for stalking prey. Today, of course, no sane hunter would wear animal skins as camo for fear of getting shot.

But decoys work for me, just as they worked for my ancestors. We're now relearning tactics they used for centuries, until they were disarmed and removed from the best hunting lands. For instance, they knew deer decoys are most effective along the edge of a field or in fairly open woods. Deer struggle to see decoys in thick woods.

How you place a deer decoy is vital for ground-based bowhunting success. The decoy must be broadside to you, with its head looking away from your position. Never place the decoy facing you when you're on the ground. If a doe or buck enters the field and notices the decoy, it will stare in the direction the decoy is looking, and then you're in trouble. Even if the deer can't see you while you're motionless, the decoy's purpose is to attract deer and divert their attention, not direct them to your hiding place. Only when their attention is focused elsewhere will you be able to easily draw your bow.

How far do you place the decoy from your blind? Because I always like to be right on top of the action, I position the decoy so I never have to shoot more than 20 yards. Ideally, my decoy is standing broadside in front of me, its head facing out into the field or possibly toward a deer trail coming out of the woods. Some hunters set the decoy farther out and angle its body differently; those are personal preferences. As long as the decoy isn't staring a hole in your setup, you should be OK.

PRICES, MODELS AND OPTIONS

In recent years, there are more decoys than ever available, from photo-realistic silhouettes to remote-controlled full-body replicas with moving heads and twitching tails. Therefore, a decoy's cost depends on how much you want to dent your billfold. They range in price from about $50 to $900.

Is the $900 full-body, mounted-deer decoy better than the $50 model? Of course it is, but you can kill deer with both.

Under the right conditions and with the right scents, cheaper decoys will work. Expensive decoys have glass eyes, an authentic tail, and realistic detail or an actual tanned deer hide. But it's not necessarily the decoy's detail that makes the magic. Its smell, demeanor and reasonably good looks are also part of the equation.

The real power, however, rests in the eye of the beholder and the buck's state of mind when he spots your decoy. When a buck is running at peak testosterone levels, and faces competition from other bucks for breeding rights to a bevy of does, the sight of your decoy might be all it takes to send him into a frenzy that brings him to your ambush site.

I've tried all sorts of decoys over the years. When using bedded decoys, I've noticed that deer often don't see them, or it's difficult for deer to make eye contact with them, and if whitetails can't see your decoy, you get no benefits, obviously. I've had better luck with standing decoys in the "I'm ready" rutting position. They're highly visible and work well for most of my hunting situations. Only you can decide which decoy is best for you.

COMMON PROBLEMS

Decoys aren't foolproof, however, and you should expect some deer to spook when spotting them, especially does and small bucks. Small bucks often spook when they think the decoy is too big and intimidating, with just too much crown atop its head. Does might not like the smell of the decoy, its posture, or lack of motion. This is where remote-control tails and heads come into their own for putting a doe at ease.

What about those small bucks? If you have no preferences regarding the bucks you'll shoot, the decoy's antlers aren't a problem. Leave the antlers in your garage and make your decoy a hot-smelling doe. That way there's no danger of your decoy showing dominance toward small bucks.

But if you're after record-book bucks, show them a hurt, inferior deer, such as a one-antlered buck. Hunters who use this trick will be rewarded, because bucks quickly notice weak inferiors, and move in to take advantage of them. A buck with only a half-crown can usually be defeated, and its rivals will try to dominate it.

Why? That's nature's way. As I often say, "Someone eats first and somebody eats last." Small, sick or injured animals are shunned or beaten down further; the strongest bucks will breed. And as long as the strong specimens do most of the breeding, the herd preserves its bloodline for future whitetails. For only the strong survive in nature's indifferent world.

REWARDS

When you're on the ground, watching how deer and other animals respond to your decoy, you'll experience fun and excitement by generating feedback from the woods' many creatures. That's why decoying is truly one of the great rewards of being a ground-pounder.

The ultimate reward, of course, comes when that decoy takes a trophy buck's eyes off your hiding place, and you come to full draw and settle that sight pin behind his shoulder. The decoy has served its purpose—attracted the interest of another whitetail and held its attention. Now it's up to you to do the rest. ■

16

PICKING UP THE PIECES

I was down, mentally and physically, after losing our farm to that 500-year flood, but I wasn't defeated. By the time autumn 1993 arrived, my need to spend time in the woods had never been greater. At least I could still bowhunt!

With our own property under water, I returned to hunt the family farm where I grew up. Even though there were no crops on the old homestead, I still believed a big whitetail might be around.

My bowhunting attention soon focused on three oak-covered ridges that came together after descending into the bottoms. I knew a good buck bedded in that area, because I jumped a buck every time I tried bowhunting one of those three ridges.

As the archery deer season headed toward late November, the weather turned terrible, with little besides ice and snow greeting each bowhunt. When I entered the woods one day, the glazed leaves and twigs gave away anything that moved, whether it was a squirrel or a bird.

Even though her thoughts in autumn 1993 never strayed far from the Great Flood and their deluged farm, Judy Kovar still went bowhunting whenever possible. She knew bucks like these had survived the floodwaters by staying in nearby hills.

I had been using a decoy and hunting from a ground blind throughout the month, but decided to try something dramatically different this day. After giving it some thought, I still-hunted through the heart of the main bedding area. I moved fast enough to sound like a deer, and in 20 minutes I was at the far end, where I found a huge scrape. I went straight to work, hanging a buck's tarsal gland as high as I could reach. Next, I poured buck urine into the scrape and onto the bark of the scrape tree. I then backed off, bow in hand, and stood within two feet of the scrape, leaning into a tree to break up my outline.

Everything was set, so I gave four or five soft grunts and waited. Within 20 minutes, there came a buck! But he didn't do what I expected. He followed a ravine toward a nearby field.

I had to act fast, so I ran to where I could get a shot. I was making a lot of noise, which he heard. But he must have mistaken me for another deer, because suddenly he turned and came straight at me! I was out in the open with nowhere to hide.

Now, the buck realized something wasn't right. He blew and trotted off. I then did the first thing that came to mind, and asked the Lord for help!

"Please make him stop. Just make him stop, and I'll do the rest!" I pleaded.

And just like that, the buck stopped! I drew my bow quickly and released the arrow.

Off he ran. My heart sank as snowflakes started falling. I was hunting alone that day, and I soon lost the blood trail. The snow kept coming down, and all I could do was walk a loop around the field and the snow-covered grass. Nothing!

I looped the field again and suddenly found tracks and blood. As I looked down the ridgetop trail, I thought I could see a rack. My heart raced, but I made myself look at the blood trail, just to make sure. I followed the tracks and blood to the buck's warm body.

Tears of relief and success spilled down my cheeks as I returned home to get Herman. The buck field-dressed 250 pounds, and I felt so satisfied to have stayed after this wonderful creature, with no thought of giving up. I'm sure part of my determination is hard-headedness, but I respect these animals and was taught to believe I owe them my best effort.

THE ESSENCE OF TIME

Good bowhunters know you can't just go into the woods and have everything go your way. Selective bowhunting for trophy whitetails takes hours, days, weeks, months and years of a good hunter's time. It all adds up, with the experiences accumulating a wealth of knowledge. For some of us, it's like a full-time job, 365 days a year.

I realize not everyone has the free time Herman and I can usually devote to bowhunting. Most bowhunters are working overtime and straight shifts to support their families, and that restricts hunting time. My only hope for all bowhunters is that they never give up this great activity. Ideally, all of us will one day get more vacation time or retire from our jobs so we can study whitetails daily, and experiment with scrapes, scents and rub lines. But if you cannot spend more time in the woods, then every moment you get must be made special.

In spring and summer, make mock scrapes and hang a dripper of urine. Whitetails investigate scrapes year-round, not just in the fall. If you can keep that scrape fresh and smelling right, you can make your mock scrapes "must-see" sites for most deer in the area. Come autumn, you'll always have popular places to bowhunt. Remember, where whitetails visit and "make their mark," others will follow.

The author arrowed this buck Nov. 27, 1993, after changing tactics. She had been decoying and rattling from a ground blind, but that day she still-hunted through a bedding area, found a scrape, doctored it and started calling. When this buck, her fifth Pope & Young trophy, headed toward an adjacent field through a ravine, she sneaked into the field to intercept it.

It's never too early to start scouting and preparing for next bow season. During winter, get out and scout new areas and look for rubs and rub lines. If you don't get to scout until spring, no problem. Just get out there! When you find last fall's rubs, and the gray, healing rubs from the year before, take note. If you find sheds, or your scouting cameras reveal these bucks are still alive, you can almost bet the farm they will be back this fall.

If you need to build a permanent tree stand, or prepare a good ground blind, anytime from winter through summer are good times for it. You want that new, treated lumber to take on color and lose some of its chemical odors.

Late spring and summer are also good times to work with farmers as they cut hay. If it's your land or you're on great terms with them regarding the use of their land, ask them to leave some bales in strategic spots where you can waylay bucks crossing or feeding in fields. By placing those blinds in summer, they'll become just another part of the whitetail's landscape.

Whenever possible, don't build a tree stand or prepare a ground blind during or right before the season. Whitetails are curious, but they're not dumb. They notice everything in their home area, especially when certain two-legged predators start running all over the late-summer woodlot, pounding boards into trees!

TIME, KNOWLEDGE AND HABITAT

To consistently shoot record-book whitetails, you have three basic needs: time, knowledge and good habitat. If deer can't find sanctuary and good nutrition where you hunt, most likely few or no record-book bucks live there.

Without good sanctuary cover, bucks seldom live long enough to grow big antlers. And if nutrition is lacking, even mature deer fall short of their potential. Their bodies use every bit of excess nutrition to maintain their skeleton, muscles

It's never too early to start scouting and preparing for next bow season. Each winter, try to scout new areas to look for rubs, scrapes, rub lines, and any other evidence of big whitetails. Sometimes you might find that a big buck you were watching won't be there come fall.

and organs, leaving little to maximize their antlers.

I like to scout fields during late summer, when it's possible to glass big bucks as they feed. I also make note of any big bucks crossing a road at night. If I'm lucky enough to spot a trophy buck, I try to figure out the best place to ambush him. I then find the landowner and discuss getting permission to bowhunt the property. Be careful about revealing the big buck's presence. Some landowners might suddenly decide they're going to hunt after all, or maybe they'll "save" the buck for their friends who gun-hunt there.

The more you scout, and the more deer sign you find, the more you learn about the land and the whitetails living there. You can't scout with maps and aerial photographs alone. They're aids only, not an answer-book. You must put in some ground time! Your knowledge of deer and the land reveal yet another important circle. Without understanding both equally, you'll never fully understand the other, and vice versa.

Plus you never know how or when the information will pay off. The only thing certain is that the more time you spend in the woods, the greater your chances of success.

This brings us to the 1997 archery season, which produced another memorable buck for me.

Indian Summer's warm winds were still blowing over Illinois' cornfields when I grabbed my burlap camo blind and headed to a farm owned by the local game warden. After hiking up a long ridge to a cluster of persimmon and ironwood trees in the late afternoon, I set the blind up quickly.

When I stepped back to inspect and admire my work, I caught movement near a dam beside a dry pond not far away. A buck stepped into the open, tested the wind, and worked his way into a grove of trees. Then I heard a noise behind me. I turned to see a doe with her two fawns. I didn't have my bow, but I stayed until dark to see what else might unfold, and to ensure I could sneak out without spooking the deer.

I had a good feeling about that ridge. It seemed to be a special place. I returned the next week and started hunting that spot in earnest. Over the next couple of weeks, I saw at least four bucks in the Pope & Young class, plus two that might have made Boone & Crockett. One 10-pointer moved within a few feet of me. Just seeing such quality bucks kept my adrenaline pumping, but none offered the shot I wanted. I knew it was only a matter of time before I got my chance.

THE CEDAR RUBS

By the time November arrived, scrapes had sprouted everywhere and bucks were chasing does. I moved my ground blind down the ridge to the edge of an opening in the woods. On the morning of November 10, 1997, I spotted a white-faced 10-pointer crossing a deep hollow behind me. Soon, snapping brush drew my attention to three small cedar trees nearby. A 4-pointer and tight-racked 6-pointer walked from the hollow and started rubbing the cedars.

Suddenly, both ran away. As I wondered what spooked them, a big-bodied buck stepped into the clearing. His ears were laid back, and he aggressively advanced on the cedars where the two smaller bucks had been rubbing. He then thrashed the cedars, literally destroying one of them.

By this time I was trembling with excitement and anticipation, but I was analyzing the situation. If he headed my way, I would have to draw my bow while seated, and be fully drawn before he topped the ridge.

I whispered an old Indian prayer to myself: "Give me strength to pull this bow back and steady my shaking arms as I wait. Then blow favorably on the feathers and make my arrow fly straight and true."

Moments later, as if by script, the buck turned and headed up the ridge. I drew, anchored and slowly stood. He glanced my way just as I released the arrow. The shaft and broadhead disappeared deeply into his chest. He almost fell, but then gathered himself and crashed away.

After I saw him disappear into the woods, I began trembling as I thanked the Great Spirit for blessing me. Then I quietly left the blind and headed home. The shot had looked good, but I wanted to make sure the sharp broadhead had time do its work undisturbed. Plus, I wanted to get Herman and have him help me track and recover the buck.

Herman and a dear friend, Chris Green, soon returned with me to the blind. I showed them where the buck had stood 17 yards away when I shot. We found my red-streaked arrow a few yards away. The blood sign was sparse at first, but just

You never know when information you've picked up from scouting will pay off. The author had a good feeling about a long ridgeline with a cluster of persimmon and ironwood trees in November 1997. She set up her ground blind and decoy, and hunted the site in earnest, eventually arrowing this big 8-pointer.

inside the woods we found large crimson splashes. Chris climbed atop a bulldozed slash pile for a better view.

"Judy, over here!" he shouted. "I see your buck. He didn't make it 30 yards into the woods."

PIECING TOGETHER A PUZZLE

Tears welled in my eyes as I thanked the Great Spirit once again. Herman and Chris hugged me and offered heartfelt congratulations. The 8-pointer weighed 220 pounds field-dressed, and later was officially scored at 128-3/8 inches, which made him my sixth whitetail for the Pope & Young records.

I had been picking up the pieces of my circle's puzzle and they were again laying a strong foundation for my future. ■

17

TRACKING TIPS FOR WHITETAILS

You have done all your homework. Your decoy or mock scrape is generating deer activity, the wind is perfect, and the buck has come in and offered a broadside shot.

But when you release your arrow, it strikes the deer where you didn't aim. You wait the allotted time and then follow a sparse blood trail. Before long you've lost the blood trail and don't know where to look next.

It's time to do everything in your power to unravel that deer's escape route!

Realize from the start that whitetails have a tremendous will to live. I've watched them turn, bite down on a protruding arrow shaft and pull it out. I've also watched them rub against a tree in an attempt to extract the arrow. They're fatally

Once your arrow strikes a whitetail, you're forever linked to that animal. Responsible bowhunters exhaust every possibility when tracking wounded deer, doing everything they can to unravel the deer's escape route.

hit, but you wouldn't know it during their initial burst of flight, which is sometimes fueled by an adrenaline surge. Herman and I have found whitetails whose hearts were cleaved nearly in half by a broadhead, yet they traveled almost unbelievable distances.

The skills needed for tracking wounded whitetails are as old as mankind itself, and they remain mostly untouched by technological aids. Good trackers rely heavily on their eyes, fingers, nose, body and soul. Bowhunters must give much of themselves to succeed, and intelligently interpret everything they spot.

If possible, don't start down the blood trail until you've found, and carefully analyzed, your arrow. That arrow can provide lots of vital information, including where it struck the deer, the depth it penetrated the body cavity, and what it encountered along its path through the deer. Study the blood, hairs, fat, tissue and other matter along the shaft.

Spend extra time studying the arrow's evidence-gathering fletchings, which is why Herman and I use feathers, not plastic vanes. Besides being more forgiving in flight, feathers gather more information while passing through a deer, making it easier to read the sign. Quite simply, blood, tissue and stomach matter soak into feathers, making for more complete analysis. We also prefer white or light-colored feathers for easier reading and interpretation. Dark feathers soak up sign, but it's more difficult to read that sign against the darker backgrounds.

When an arrow holds stomach matter, it's usually obvious what happened, but never overlook your shot angle. If your arrow sliced through the abdomen on its way in or out of the deer's chest cavity, you'll find evidence of a gut shot even though the deer will die quickly from its chest hemorrhage.

If you arrow breaks, look inside the shaft for lung tissue, hairs, hide, fat tissue or residue from the stomach, liver or bone marrow. What color is the hair? Don't just look at it. Analyze it. What is it trying to tell you? If it's white, it's belly hair. If it's brown with black tips, it's likely from the flanks.

Until the evidence suggests otherwise, always assume you made a fatal shot. Don't quit without a good search! Quitters disgrace the animal by dishonoring the hunt. Give of yourself, prove yourself, and find that deer!

If your arrow passed through the deer, study the broadhead closely. As with fletching, broadheads collect lots of good information. Although they usually contain dirt from where you pull them from the ground, they still usually hold body tissues, hair, tendon, bone chips or muscle tissue.

Until the evidence heavily suggests otherwise, always assume you made a fatal shot. Don't quit without a good search! Quitters disgrace the animal by dishonoring the hunt. Give of yourself, prove yourself, and find that deer!

The author always lives by a goal she set during her early days of bowhunting in the 1980s: One arrow, one deer. She arrowed this 8-pointer during the 1988 Illinois archery season.

ON THE TRAIL

Once you start tracking, bear down on the job and do more than search for blood. Look for tracks or sliding marks in the leaves. Many times a wounded whitetail will favor its injured side and leave deeper impressions and tracks on its opposite hoof. Upon finding such tracks, you'll know you're still in the game.

If the ground is too dry for hoofs to penetrate, and blood is the only sign you can follow, your challenge definitely increases.

Don't be quickly discouraged if blood is sparse the first few yards. Many tree-stand bowhunters hit one lung, but the shot angle doesn't always allow a pass-through. If the arrow doesn't exit the deer's undercarriage, you shouldn't be surprised if blood sign is slow at first. Blood must fill the lung until it reaches the entrance hole, and then pump out and to the ground. This process doesn't happen instantly, so be patient as you trail that animal.

If you can't find tufts of hair, snapped twigs, broken grass or weeds, pull out your small bottle of hydrogen peroxide. No matter how small or old a blood spot, when a light spray of peroxide hits it, blood foams. I once sprayed a five-square-foot area, thinking it might hold the key to which direction my buck moved. The spray foamed up, showing me the buck had backtracked.

Granted, spraying leaves with hydrogen peroxide is painstaking work, but you

Whitetails are like us and respond differently as individuals, and as circumstances change. That's why the author cringes when someone begins a sentence with, "Whitetails always . . . " The truth is, when it comes to whitetail behavior, you can't make foolproof predictions.

owe it to the animal to try everything. Plus, hydrogen peroxide is inexpensive and works well except in downpours, when blood gets diluted. On the other extreme, I've sprayed dry blood that is days old and it still foamed and showed me the way.

As you unravel the trail, take extra time to look for sign on both sides of fences along the deer's path. Study every track you find, analyzing its depth and length. If you find skid marks, the deer might be struggling to stand or walk. Wounded whitetails often walk in a circle, stand, listen and watch, trying to determine the situation before jumping over fences and other obstacles. By finding evidence of indecision and hesitancy to jump, you can determine if that deer had the energy to leap over a fence, gate or ditch.

If you decide your deer jumped the obstacle, try to determine if it landed on all fours. Is it favoring a leg or shoulder? If so, the other three hoofs will support more weight and leave a deeper impression.

Also study every deer bed you find along your search route. If a wounded deer lies down, see if it left blood and hair. If you find blood clots, study their color and consistency. Are they big and thick? If so, the deer will need to make a new clot and will likely bleed heavily again until the clot forms.

What if the clots are thin and small? You might be in trouble. The wound is probably swelling and slowing the blood flow. Either that or the deer's hide is moving as it walks, covering the wound now and then. Such signs indicate an increasingly difficult search.

EXPECT THE UNEXPECTED

Again, though, keep searching for evidence in every way possible. Injured whitetails can—and will—do unusual things, and not all wounded deer head downhill. I've had hard-hit whitetails climb steep hills, and I've seen lightly scratched whitetails choose the easiest paths possible. Again, whitetails are like us and respond differently as individuals, and as circumstances change. That's why I cringe when someone begins a sentence with, "Whitetails always . . . " The truth is, when it comes to whitetail behavior, you can't make foolproof predictions.

Sometimes even the best trackers read too much into the sign. Herman and I have followed long blood trails so red that we almost guaranteed each other we would find the deer over the next rise. In fact, one whitetail we tracked down traveled more than two miles over wooded ridges, never stopping for water, even though we were certain the shot had been on target. That great-looking shot, complete with lots of air bubbles on bloodstained leaves, turned out to be a sliced diaphragm, not a lung shot.

Speaking of which, be careful when you find air bubbles in the blood. Blood from a chest wound doesn't necessarily contain air bubbles. In the best-case scenarios, bubbly pink blood indicates the deer is aspirating lung blood through its nose and mouth, which means it won't go far. In many cases, however, bubbles form when air gets trapped beneath blood as it hits leaves. That's why some hunters think they're looking at lung blood when it actually came from muscle tissue.

Be careful when interpreting blood color. The amount of time that passes from when you shoot to when you find the blood affects its color, whether it falls on leaves, grass or twigs. Blood can also soak into wood and blend into the grain. When Herman and I were following a diaphragm-hit buck, we lost the trail several times. Once the buck walked through the branches of a dead elm tree. With no blood to follow, we sat down atop the fallen tree trunk to ponder our next move.

When I glanced alongside him, I noticed a fresh scratch on the tree trunk. The scratch suggested the buck was losing strength and its hoofs hadn't cleared the trunk. Next, I noticed a couple of tiny spots, but they were dry and didn't look like blood. I flicked at the spots and my fingers revealed damp blood. Within minutes we were back on the buck's trail.

HONOR THE ANIMAL

At some point, unfortunately, every hunter experiences the heartache of a lost animal. Even after a few days pass, keep looking. If nothing else, you might retrieve the buck's head and find a place to honor it in your home.

A few minutes before twilight, go out and listen for howling coyotes. If you hear fighting and howling, they might be feeding on a deer's carcass. At dawn, listen for crows. They also make a lot of noise when feeding on a carcass and fighting over scraps. In other words, these creatures are giving you one last chance to find your deer.

Granted, depending on how long it's been dead, what you find will not resemble the beautiful creature you shot. Even so, find another cape and do those antlers justice.

As Grey Wolf would say, "Listen to the wind, for it carries the cries of many (coyotes, crows, hawks and eagles). Listen with all your heart and hunt like the warrior. Use everything around you. It's there for your journey."

All bowhunters choose many different paths each autumn. Some are blood trails that bring the joys of a bountiful hunt. Others simply test our skills and determination. ■

18

A PREMATURE DEATH CHANT

As the first freeze of 1994 nipped the leaves and stole their brilliant September colors, I knew another bowhunting season was near. Herman and I made plans on which areas to hunt first and where to build new blinds. Herman also mentioned my health and suggested I visit the county health department for my annual flu shot. I didn't want to get sick during the season, so I agreed to go the next day.

Judy Kovar arrowed this chocolate-phase black bear in spring 1995 while bowhunting in Saskatchewan. Only six months before, after being struck by a strange illness, she was told she might not live to see the next dawn. Photo courtesy: Judd Cooney.

Meanwhile, Herman had learned from a friend in southern Illinois that a special bowhunt was about to open. He hadn't hunted down there for years, so we agreed he should go. The next morning I drove into town, got my flu shot, and then returned to help Herman pack.

I had received flu shots before, so I didn't suspect any link seven hours later when my right eye and right cheek began feeling strange. Herman was concerned, but I knew he was also eager to hit the road. I figured I was probably just catching a little cold or sinus congestion, so I encouraged him to leave. With my assurances that I was fine, he climbed

The author's bout of Bells Palsey made her again realize how many good people she had met through archery and bowhunting. One of the first people to call to check up on her was M.R. James, founder and editor emeritus of Bowhunter magazine.

into his Bronco and disappeared down the road.

But my condition soon worsened. My right eye wouldn't close and it watered constantly. Then the right side of my mouth dropped. I couldn't drink soda from a glass or can. The liquid spilled out faster than I could swallow it. My head suddenly hurt terribly. The pain was almost more than I could stand, and I couldn't control my right arm.

What was happening? Suddenly I realized I shouldn't have let Herman go hunting! My mind raced. My mother had suffered a stroke the year before. Could I be suffering one, too? I didn't want to take a chance, so I called the doctor's office and hurried into town.

Our family doctor wasn't in, so one of his associates examined me. After looking me over and hearing about my mother's history, she said I should hurry to the hospital's emergency room. When I again asked what was wrong, she told me to call my husband and get my affairs in order. She didn't think I would make it through the night!

I had heard enough. I decided it was time to go home. I asked how much I owed.

"Where do you think you're going?" she asked.

I told her if I was going to die, I'd rather be in peace at home with my pipe, bow, arrows, whitetail mounts and buffalo robe. Why go to a hospital and run up a huge bill for Herman?

When I arrived home after the 30-plus mile drive, I heard our phone ringing as I slid my key into the door. I grabbed the phone and recognized the voice of our family doctor. He asked why I hadn't gone to the hospital. I explained that I didn't need a hospital if I was doomed.

He then told me I wasn't going to die, and that my stroke-like symptoms were probably Bells Palsy, which had been triggered by the flu shot. Even so, I had to brace for uncertainty. The doctor couldn't guarantee everything would return to normal.

ON THE TRAIL

Meanwhile, after hearing from my doctor's office, Illinois conservation wardens went out hunting for Herman. When they found him and explained what they knew, he jumped back into the Bronco and hit the gas. Unfortunately, at that point everyone thought I had suffered a stroke and was dying. Herman raced for the hospital, not knowing that I had ignored that plan.

About two hours after I returned home, M.R. James called, asking what was happening. Despite my predicament, I felt deeply touched by his concern and again marveled at my friendships within the archery family.

Herman, meanwhile, went straight to the hospital and rushed inside. I can only imagine the look on his face when he learned I wasn't there! He then rushed back to the truck and raced for home. These were the days before cellular phones were common, and he didn't want to waste time looking for a pay phone.

A short while after I talked to M.R., I saw Herman turn into our driveway and I waited for him to walk in. When the door opened, his face said it all. I looked bad. We calmly and quietly discussed the problem and our possible solutions.

Herman understood my feelings and why I had come home. That evening as I lay by his side with his arms around me, I felt at ease and ready to accept whatever the Creator decided. When I looked outside, I saw the night sky held no stars, and no moon glistened in the distance. I tried to sleep but feared what dawn might bring.

My thoughts turned to Grey Wolf. "Oh Grandfather, where are you? Do you look upon me now? Where will this path take me? If I close my eyes will they open in the morning?"

Herman and I finally drifted into sleep, neither of us knowing what to expect. When I awoke the next morning, Herman put his hand on my forehead and then my throat. He asked how I felt.

The next few weeks were a struggle. I refused to go out in public because I didn't want anyone to see me. My face was terribly distorted and would scare children. I had to call several school districts and cancel presentations. No amount of Herman's encouragement could get me out of the house.

Get-well cards and letters from fellow bowhunters across the United States helped boost my spirits and bolstered my strength and courage to beat the illness. Weekly calls from M.R. and Dr. Dave Samuel gave me quick pick-me-ups, and I wished they weren't so far away. They both suggested I try bowhunting a few hours, just to get out of the house. I tried but my right eye wouldn't focus and it watered constantly. My right hand also trembled terribly, and trying to bring the bow to full draw seemed impossible. Herman coaxed me daily, sometimes with the tongue of a serpent, but I refused to let him lower my bow's poundage.

And so the 1994 bowhunting season passed by without me. Even though my health gradually returned and I was on the road to recovery, we still didn't know how long the journey would last.

The autumn 1994 archery season went on without Judy Kovar. She tried to shoot her bow, but her right eye wouldn't focus and it watered constantly. Her right hand trembled terribly. Trying to draw her bow proved impossible.

SPRING RETURNS

As the months passed and my condition steadily improved, I began to make plans once more. The Pope & Young Club was holding a banquet and awards presentation that year, so I decided to donate a handmade elk-hide wedding dress for the club's auction. The P&Y Club had believed in me, and my public school presentations, when few others had, so I thought I should give something back.

I called M.R. James and told him I needed to make this contribution to the Club to show my appreciation for all of its support. I'm sure M.R. also knew I needed the challenge for my own well-being. The 1994 archery season had been one long frustration with no deer. I was now ready mentally and physically to be myself again. I wanted to greet the world and the people who stood by me. I wanted to thank those who had called, sent flowers and telephoned encouraging words.

Finally, departure day arrived and we boarded a plane to the P&Y convention. When we arrived, the sight of our many friends renewed my energy. During the auction, Herman talked to outdoor writer and outfitter Judd Cooney, and discussed the possibility of bowhunting black bears in Canada. Herman told Judd that I would want to hunt from the ground, but he was concerned for my safety. Judd assured Herman he would stay with me for protection if needed.

When we returned home, we sent Judd our license fees, not realizing a new battle was surfacing. My arm was still a mess, and drawing the bow and holding it at full draw any length of time was impossible. In fact, I often could not get the bow to break over. I just couldn't shoot my usual 62 pounds anymore. I finally let Herman back the new bow down to 52 pounds. I could now pull it back, but I needed new arrows.

Within the week, I was hitting the target at 15 yards. Still, I was not myself. The illness seemed to feast daily on our marriage and my mental state, and it affected my bowhunting ability, too. Suddenly, I was so afraid that I wrote my will, and I didn't plant flowers in front of the house that spring. I figured if I passed and Herman took up with a new woman or wife, I wasn't going to plant flowers for her to enjoy!

The author poses with her trophy bear. She remembers releasing the string and watching the hot-pink fletching disappear into the chocolate fur. The beast simply turned and walked off, but Judy saw her bloodied arrow sticking in the dirt embankment beyond.

The day before we left for Canada, M.R. James called and tried to ease my fears. "Just think, Judy," he said. "You're going to see bears from a perspective no one else will ever see!"

BEARS AT EYE LEVEL

We arrived at Judd's camp in Canada on May 14, 1995. We discussed our hunt that night while seated around a fire, and Judd asked what kind of bear I wanted to arrow. I laughed and said, "The first one I see before he eats me!"

Judd told me about a bear in the bogs that was an interesting chocolate-color phase, and said it was borderline book material. The next afternoon, Judd and I traveled the gravel road toward the bait site and then slipped into the blind. I studied the blind and looked back at Judd.

The blind consisted of three or four pieces of a jack pine stuck into the ground, and Judd had me standing in front of them. The only thing between me and the bait barrel was an aspen tree about three inches in diameter.

Judd then told me good luck and climbed into his tree stand! What happened to the guy who promised to stay there to protect me?

Now alone, I stood at full alert. I was sure I was a goner every time a leaf rustled! Plus the mosquitoes were so bad, I could barely see out of my face mask. And then I heard twigs snapping and I knew my moment of truth was near. From my left walked the biggest chocolate bear I had ever seen. His body jiggled as he walked, and his fur was thick and sleek.

The bear walked in front of the bait site and then paused to listen while standing broadside in front of the barrel and me. I raised my bow and tried to pull it back, but I couldn't do it! Worse, the bear noticed my movements. I looked to Judd for a signal, but he was reading a book! The bear turned and laid his ears back. The fur on the back of his neck rose toward the sky, and his front legs bounced with energy.

Judd was now paying attention, and he realized the bear was about to charge.

The author enjoyed getting back into the woods in spring 1995 after her frightening illness, even if it meant battling Canada's notorious mosquitoes. Here she gets a ride back to camp with one of Judd Cooney's guides, Mike Kraetsch. Photo courtesy: Judd Cooney.

Unfortunately, he didn't have time to grab his shotgun. All he could do was crease the page he was reading, close the book and watch. He later said he would have thrown the book at the bear as it ran past his stand to eat me!

When I stopped moving, the bear settled back into its quest for something to eat. The big boar sat down and stuck his huge paw into the barrel. I now brought my bow back up and tried again to draw. With my last bit of energy and with silent prayers on my lips, I broke the bow over and put my sight pin just behind the bear's shoulder. I shook my head in one last attempt to rid the face mask of mosquitoes, but only a few fell.

I settled the single pin one final time behind the great beast's shoulder. I remember releasing the string and watching the hot-pink fletching disappear into the chocolate fur. The beast simply turned and walked off, but I saw my arrow and its bloodstained fletching sticking in the dirt embankment.

I looked to Judd, and he gave me a thumbs-up. I shook as the adrenaline drained from my body, and I started to fall. At the same time I heard the death bawl, and I wondered if the big bear was truly dead or just mad.

I kept waiting for Judd to come over, and looked one last time as I fell to my knees. I then grabbed for the small aspen as I went down. The trees were spinning and I felt queasy, so I held onto the aspen and waited for Judd.

He finally reached my side and congratulated me. "Now let's go see your bear," Judd said excitedly. "He's right over there! He didn't even go 30 feet!"

Judd grabbed my left hand, which encircled the tree, but my hand refused to release. He patted my hand and again tried to get me to release the tree. I looked at him and said I couldn't get up.

"You're . . . you're . . . you're having a heart attack, aren't you?" Judd asked.

"No," my legs just won't stay under me," I said.

He finally pried my fingers from the tree, and we walked arm-in-arm over to where my first bear lay on the ground. I had done it the way my grandfather once did: Up close and one-on-one.

I leaned down and touched the bear's huge head and chest. I again fell to my knees, but this time I gave thanks to the Creator. My mind raced with all kinds of feelings and emotions, and my tears fell onto the bear's great muzzle. The two of us had come together for a brief moment and we shared a common spirit. Bears have always been special to my people. We admire their strength, courage and will to live. I had indeed become one with this bear.

NEWFOUND RESPECT

When Judd and I returned to camp, Herman and the others were sitting around the fire. Floyd, one of the Indian guides, had told Herman of my success.

Judd told everyone, "I watched Judy after she arrowed that bear, and saw her go to her knees. I didn't want to bother her because I thought she was doing some kind of Indian prayer." We all laughed!

Whenever I think about that special day, I recall my renewed respect for my ancestors. I'm filled with awe by the way they hunted, realizing they often went up against noble bears one-on-one with a bow. I now better appreciate how they looked an animal in the eye, and for a moment shared the spirit of the Old Ones and their courage.

Bowhunting bears from the ground is definitely rewarding. Grandfather had told me legendary stories about the bear, and I remember my childhood, when I played on a bearskin robe and touched the bear-claw necklace around Grandfather's weathered neck.

Later, as I lay between sheets smelling faintly of sweet grass and burning white sage, I thought one night about all that I had been through from fall 1994 through late spring 1995. Then I drifted off to sleep and found myself filled with strange visions or dreams. I later tried to dismiss those dreams, little realizing how important they would be.

My life, my path, was again about to change. ■

19

TICKET TO A TREETOP CAT

As with many things, memorable bowhunts often start as a wish, a dream, or some other random thought. In fact, one of my most unforgettable hunts began with a raffle ticket.

In 1995, Herman and I traveled to Traverse City, Michigan, to attend the Pope

A winning lottery ticket at the Pope & Young Club's convention in 1995 sent the author to Montana a year later to hunt mountain lions. In December 1996, she shot this 175-pound cat, which has a Pope & Young score of 14-13/16. It was 8-1/2 years old and ranks as the largest mountain lion taken by a female bowhunter.

& Young Club's convention and banquet. We arrived early to see the sights, admire the trophies on display, and renew old friendships with Club members. One of those friends, Don Dvoroznak of Thompson Falls, Montana, approached and asked if we wanted to buy a raffle ticket for some great bowhunts and/or float trips down the Yellowstone River. Herman gave Don a $20 bill for our ticket, and then wrote my name and phone number on the entry stub.

Months went by and we forgot about the raffle. Then, when we returned home one day, we heard Don's excited voice on our answering machine. When I returned his call, he said: "Kiddo, you won the mountain lion hunt in Montana from Jerry Malson Outfitting. Its total value is worth more than $3,000." Don congratulated me and said Jerry would be in touch soon.

Herman looked at me and shook his head. "That's what I get for putting your name on the ticket instead of mine!" he said. "What a hunt this is going to be."

When Jerry and I spoke, he said I needed to be in Montana by December 1. Unfortunately, this was 1995, and Father died in November of that year. I had no choice but to cancel the lion hunt and stay home to sort out family business and care for Mother. Herman and I rescheduled our Montana lion trip for December 1996.

When November 1996 arrived and the Illinois woods came alive with rutting bucks, we marveled once more at the morning frosts and steadily falling leaves. Even so, my daydreams seldom strayed far from the Montana lion hunt. I was excited, but also worried. Could I do it? What kind of physical endurance would I need? Could I take the cold and hold on for long rides on a snowmobile? Then I heard that a camera crew was joining us to videotape my hunt for a Minnesota television show. Would I be able to handle the added pressure of having my every move videotaped?

COLD DOUBTS

When we pulled into Jerry's place on December 3, my worries eased a bit. Jerry greeted us as if we were family, and filled us in on what to expect. The next day we went out with our guides, Speed and George, and soon got a close-up look at a lion. When that lion grew tired of the hounds and bailed out of the tree, it landed only a few feet from us. As it streaked by, passing within two feet of us, it looked at us as if we were mere obstacles.

Unfortunately, the weather was terrible, and the region was receiving six to eight inches of snow every day or evening. By the third day of hunting, December 6, I was feeling down. The snow added to the challenge of going anywhere, even in four-wheel-drive trucks. From there, breaking a trail on foot through ever-deepening snow proved more difficult each time the hounds treed a cat. All the while, cold air and sharp winds never eased, but we continued.

By late morning that day, we arrived at the bottom of the McCully Ridge territory. George was worried about Speed and his whereabouts, and kept calling for him on the CB radio. Finally, our radio crackled to life with Speed's excited voice:

"I'm running down the road. I think the dogs are running parallel with the ridge and just went over McCully Ridge. If they did, we're going to have to

Chasing mountain lions in December in Montana is no easy endeavor. The mountainous country received six- to eight-inch snowfalls daily during the author's bowhunt.

snowmobile in and break trail until we reach them. Get the younger dogs ready and load them on the sled. I'll be there pretty soon. We'll try to find the dogs. They're now out of range."

As George opened the latches of the dog boxes, I asked the location of McCully Ridge.

"You see that mountain way ahead of us?" he asked. "The dogs ran over it. We'll have to snowmobile over the top just to get to the dogs."

I strained to look through the thick fog ahead. Finally, I saw the top of the snow-covered range and my heart fluttered as I realized its enormous size. George then left, telling us to wait for his return.

It seemed to take forever for George to come back, but then we quickly loaded my bow and Tim's camera equipment. Speed had stayed on site with the dogs to keep an eye on the lion. We would have to make two trips: one for me and the cameraman, and another trip for Herman and the second cameraman.

I needed all my arm strength to maintain my hold on George as the snowmobile bounced and weaved through the deep, rocky ravine. In fact, we overturned repeatedly, and I sometimes fell under the snowmobile's tracks. The trip was difficult and dangerous, but then we reached the top and descended through four to five feet of snow on the flats and ridges.

When the snowmobile finally stopped, I faintly heard the howling dogs.

George noticed my arms were shaking from the long ride, and I told him I wasn't sure I could pull the bow back. Meanwhile, Speed volunteered to go back for Herman and the cameraman. George then offered to carry my coat, and I saw doubt in his face.

PREDATOR VS. PREDATOR

We soon arrived at the tree and the younger dogs injected life into the older hounds as their voices echoed against the ravine walls. When I looked up into the branches, my eyes finally met the lion's. During that brief moment we stared at each other, I heard no dogs, only my heavy heart beats.

I saw the lion's huge paws and watched his flanks moving in and out with every breath he drew. His cold grey eyes were half-closed, and his lean body wrapped around the back side of the huge Ponderosa pine. Only when one of the cameramen moved directly under the tree did the lion take offense and snarl.

I stood before the huge cat, realizing this bowhunt pitted two predators against each other. Suddenly my eyes filled with tears as I honored the great beast. I reached into a front pocket for my tobacco bag, pinched some of its dry contents, and offered them to the winds and the lion.

Herman and Judy Kovar paused for this photo during her December 1996 bowhunt for a mountain lion. Herman was alongside her during the hunt, expressing confidence that she had the skill, strength and determination to endure the cold weather and make the tough shot.

The author's knees buckled when her guides informed her that she had just killed a mountain lion that would score very high in the Pope & Young Club's record book.

Herman had arrived by then, and he called to me. I worked my way around the dogs and snow-covered deadfalls. Herman had found the only possible shot, but it wouldn't be easy. An array of limbs and bear-hair moss obscured the lion's body. The shot window measured about three by five inches.

"This is it," Herman said. "Just take your time and stick it in there."

Speed had been looking for another shot window, but to no avail. I shared his concerns about arrow penetration, and wanted to ensure I didn't wound this huge lion. We not only had to worry about the dogs' safety, but also our own. With both cameras now rolling, I nocked my arrow and double-checked to ensure my release was attached.

Then, with all my strength, I pulled the string back and anchored. My eye found the peep and top pin, and aligned them with each other. Slowly, I raised the bow to almost a vertical angle. I heard Herman whisper, "Remember, top pin, Babe."

I now planted the sight pin on the big lion, but took my eyes off it momentarily to look at this giant predator one last time. Then I moved my head back into alignment with the sights and touched off the release. The arrow and its white and yellow feathers disappeared into the tawny body.

All hell broke loose! Limbs broke with thunderous snaps, and the lion smashed into the ground. The howling hounds strained and yanked at their ropes, which were secured to small pine trees nearby. They pulled so hard that the small trees were nearly flattened into the snow.

George and Speed stood poised with a rifle and handgun, crouching at times to stay positioned to protect us if needed. We struggled to communicate over the din of howling hounds, sometimes speaking, sometimes using hand signals. Then the lion was dead, its long tail motionless less than six yards from the tree where it had made its final stand.

A TROPHY CAT

Finally, as the commotion quieted and everyone moved in for a better look, I hugged Herman and cried.

"It looked good to me all the way," he said. "You did a good job, Babe."

After a few minutes, Speed and George gathered up the dogs and moved them away from the site. They then returned and pulled the lion into full view for everyone. Speed kept saying, "Look at that head! That's a hell of a head! He's got to make the Pope & Young records."

I cradled the lion's huge head in my hands, and studied its large body. His front paws were as big as both of my hands put together. When I asked Herman for my coat, he knew I wanted my tobacco pouch. I knelt and sprinkled pinches of tobacco over the lion's body. I wiped the tears flowing down my cheeks and rubbed them onto the cat's muzzle. I thanked the Spirits for their help and this gift. A moment had been shared by two predators whose eyes had met and whose hearts had become one. I was humbled by my quarry's courage and cunning.

The snowmobile ride back over the mountain to our vehicles took two hours. Soon after the huge lion arrived at Jerry's lodge, we took more pictures and then watched some of the TV crew's videotape.

When Herman and I finally turned in that night, I couldn't sleep. My mind continued to race. What an incredible ending to a dream hunt. No one could have foretold that a raffle ticket would produce such an event and affect so many lives. That $20 ticket not only created new acquaintances. It also produced a record-book mountain lion.

My cougar measured 81 inches from nose to tail and weighed 175 pounds. Speed estimated it was 8-1/2 years old. The skull's green score was 15-2/8, well above the Pope & Young Club's minimum. M.R. James later officially measured the dry skull, and gave it a 14-13/16-inch measurement, making it the largest lion taken in Montana by a female bowhunter.

CONCLUSION

When Herman and I were back home and sitting before our fireplace, we watched the rough cuts of videotape and remembered the hunt. Later, when Herman asked what I wanted for Christmas, I looked at him through teary eyes.

"I already have my present," I said. "I have my Christmas lion!"

I wiped away the tears and asked myself: "What does Mother think of her warrior now?" ■

20

A NEW SEASON

After Herman and I tagged bears during our spring 1995 hunt with Judd Cooney in Canada, I had high hopes for the fall deer season. The hot summer passed, and by the time October arrived I was booking presentations in the public schools almost daily.

I knew one thing for sure: The more schools I could book for presentations in early October, the more days I would have free to bowhunt in November. But life again took an unforeseen path just as I finished a round of seminars at our local schools on November 6, 1995.

That evening, Herman and I planned to meet our good friends Jerry Peterson and Gary Sefton of Wood Wise Products, who had invited us to Pike County for a whitetail banquet and management seminar. We enjoyed the banquet, but when we arrived home our answering machine was blinking with messages.

Judy Kovar's father died unexpectedly Nov. 6, 1995. Less than three months later, on Feb. 3, 1996, her mother followed. Afterward, Judy wrote, "We move our feet and walk around in our new life, but we never escape the grief of losing our loved ones." The photo of Alice Dean was taken before her marriage to Ervin P. Hamilton in 1936.

The first call was from a neighbor near my parents' house. "Please call your parents as soon as you get back!" The next message simply said, "Judy, please call the farm as soon as you get home!" The third call was from my middle daughter, pleading me to call quickly. The fourth message was from my aunt, who said how sorry she was to hear of my father's death.

I was stunned. This couldn't be happening. Mother was in a wheelchair and Father had been taking care of her for three years. What would happen now? How would I take care of Mother?

My mind whirled as Herman drove us to the farm. The next few days I functioned in a daze. I again had to cancel school presentations and couldn't reschedule them until I had arranged live-in care for Mother.

NO TIME TO BOWHUNT

The bowhunting season came and went, and I saw the woods and cornfields only five times in three months. I did see a buck that likely scored in the 170s, but family life and my commitments to Mother left little time for for me to get quality time afield to go bowhunting.

Fall faded away, and as the New Year unfolded, I continued to care for and tend to Mother, the farm and family obligations. But Mother wasn't the same without Father, and since her stroke three years before, life was not going smoothly for her. Her inability to speak and hold a conversation angered her, and she didn't like having someone caring for her in her own home.

The photo of Ervin was taken in the 1930s when he played trumpet in the Calhoun County Band in Illinois.

Herman and I found time in January 1996 to attend the Archery Trade Show for a few days of rest and to renew old friendships. But when we returned home, Mother was having problems. Her doctor said it was probably the flu, and there was little he could do. By the end of the week, Mother needed to be hospitalized for severe headaches and to undergo tests.

Early Saturday morning, February 3, a hospital nurse called and asked me to come back to try to quiet Mother, who was now on oxygen. When I entered her room, she was in pain and fighting for every breath. I talked to her and bent down to kiss her forehead. She looked at me intently. I knew what she wanted to do. Her eyes never left mine as I pulled a chair to her bedside and fluffed her pillow. I laid her head on the pillow and brushed her silver hair.

"I'm here with you, Mother," I said. "If you want to go, I understand. You know Father is waiting, don't you?"

We can think we're prepared for a loved one's passing, but when their final heartbeats send tiny ripples across the monitor and then flatten into nothingness, you're never ready.

She nodded a tearful "Yes." I held her hand and watched the heart monitor slowly flatten. A nurse came in and asked if I wanted anything. I shook my head.

"No. Mother has a living will and her wishes will be carried out."

I again looked at Mother, and told her I loved her and was there for her. She blinked her teary eyes in acknowledgment. It was so difficult to sit there and just let her go. We can think we're prepared for such moments, but when those final heartbeats send tiny ripples across the monitor and then flatten into nothingness, you're never ready. Eventually, the doctor came into the room, and at 9:30 a.m. he pronounced her dead.

The nurses who came in remarked how peaceful she looked. I had to agree.

LONELY FEARS

I fully realized I was now alone, the only one left from Grey Wolf's family to carry on what he had taught firsthand. I was afraid of tomorrow and the unseen paths I now had to follow. At least I had Herman. The circle had again closed. Again I knew I must play the warrior's role, but I was suddenly more tired than ever before.

Just before they sealed the coffin, Herman helped me lay a rope of sweetgrass in Mother's hands. We also left a bag of tobacco and an eagle feather with her, hoping her path in this circle would be complete. We asked that her voice be heard among the elders, and that she assume her rightful place beside Grandfather. We asked that the Creator and the Keeper nourish this kind woman, for her body would now nourish the earth, the originator of all life. We asked that the circle of life resume.

I fully realized I was now alone, the only one left from Grey Wolf's family to carry on what he had taught firsthand. I was afraid of tomorrow and the unseen paths I now had to follow.

"Mother, I sing your death song, and know you are again one with the earth. Watch over me as I travel down my path within this circle. Guide my daily decisions and stand by me."

I felt my legs begin to buckle and Herman was there to support me. I looked one last time at Mother. Never again would I see her tanned features or feel her loving kiss on my cheek. My heart cried for her.

She was my best friend and she always nursed me when I was ill. Yet few people knew of her and the few happy moments that flickered into her life before vanishing. Nor did many people comprehend the bond that Mother and I shared.

FAREWELL

Three months to the day after we buried Mother, I sat in her room, humming a prayer song and chanting softly. I wished I weren't an only child. I wished life wouldn't be so relentless with its heavy blows.

We move our feet and walk around in our new life, but we never escape the grief of losing our loved ones. ■

21

SHAPE-SHIFTING FOR WHITETAILS

Strong, dry winds swirled in every direction as I sat along the edge of my farm's freshly picked cornfield. All the while I questioned my decision to leave the house that afternoon in fall 2002. I had to be a bit crazy to try bowhunting in this windy, scent-spreading situation.

As I continued to question myself, a shadowy figure suddenly appeared and then vanished just as quickly. My eyes strained and searched the field edge, waiting for another glimpse. Finally, the figure stepped into the picked field. Its body was massive and its gait was more of a shuffle. With its nose to the ground, the whitetail started crossing the cornfield.

LONG TIME COMING

I was fairly certain I knew the buck's identity. The previous two seasons, I had encountered a buck nearby that tried my bowhunting skills and my fortitude. This buck also left sign that was almost scary. It rubbed huge trees, and in many cases it twisted or snapped off trees thicker than two inches in diameter. Its deep, wide tracks indicated a body weight of at least 300 pounds. In addition, a neighbor's headlights caught a glimpse of its antlers one night, which created plenty of intrigue throughout the fall. Perhaps most intriguing of all, however, was the buck's shy nature. It moved like the evening's shadows, never visible for more than a few seconds before disappearing.

I was well into season No. 3 with this buck when it crossed that picked cornfield. Then again, maybe I could trace this shadowy buck's bloodline back as far as 13 years. One cold, snowy day, I had been taking the kids to school when I spotted a huge antler in the middle of the road. The right-hand shed was stained with fresh blood, and it carried impressive mass and tine length throughout. For the next three weeks I combed every field, ravine, bedding area and creek bank for the matching left antler, but to no avail.

The seasons came and went, and I heard a few rumors about others seeing a massive buck, but those stories were as elusive as the buck itself.

Finally, in more recent years, I spotted a buck whose antler characteristics matched that old shed I'd found in the road. I was glassing a field when I spotted a massive buck feeding in the corn stubble. Then, one evening during the early bow season the next year, I spooked seven deer into the woods as I approached my

The author poses with her seventh Pope & Young whitetail, which she arrowed November 6, 2002. The 11-point nontypical scored 146 points. To arrow this trophy buck, Judy wore a Sleeping Indian's Shape Shifter suit over a Scent-Lok suit and then hid in tall weeds along the edge of a cut cornfield.

ground blind. The last deer did not run like the others. When I glassed the shadowy figure, I noticed the crown of large antlers atop its head.

Obviously, I'll never know for sure if these bucks of different eras were from the same gene pool, but their antler traits certainly suggested a shared heritage. I bowhunted often during that 2001 Illinois season, but didn't get another glimpse of the shadowy buck. I was more ready than ever when the 2002 archery season opened October 1.

CHANGE OF TACTICS

Still, I wasn't able to verify the buck as the season unfolded. One night I thought I was close, but all I could do was listen as a buck grunted and chased a doe just below the lip of a dam forming a small millpond.

In my mind, I stepped back and tried to view the situation objectively. My instincts told me no tree stand or ground blind would give me the drop on this buck where he usually moved. When Herman and I talked about it after I returned home, he offered to rattle or grunt-call for me if I thought it would help. I said I'd think about it.

That evening I was browsing through the latest hunting catalog when I noticed an old-time sniper/ghillie suit and a Sleeping Indian's wool camo Shape Shifter suit. A new strategy started unfolding in my mind. Eight years before, Ted Ranck, owner of Sleeping Indian, had sewed me a custom set of clothing.

This photo shows how effectively the Shape Shifter outfit disguises the author in tall weeds, which are common along the edges of Midwestern agricultural fields.

I quickly looked up Ted's phone number and called. We talked and reminisced, and then I told him about my latest challenge. I said I wanted to order one of his Shape Shifter suits, so he took down the necessary measurements and asked whether I wanted grey or brown wool. I picked his mixture of both colors, because of my farm/field hunting sites. Ted said my suit would be on the way within the next day.

I felt like a kid waiting for Christmas. I wasted little time trying on the suit when it arrived. I had my arms in and the hood up quickly, and

Herman told me to turn around a couple of times and then walk around. He was impressed.

"That's awesome, Judy," he said. "Now go shape-shift that monster buck."

Herman added that he had only one concern: "I hope no one mistakes you for Bigfoot or Sasquatch and shoots you."

He was joking, but it's interesting he made that connection. Many Native American tribes, such as the Pueblo, Zuni and Sioux, use the term "shape shifter" because they believe some special tribal members can change their appearance or bodies with their animal brothers.

The second day I wore the Shape Shifter outfit to bowhunt the Shadow, I placed my decoy near my setup at the field's edge in tall weeds, and then laid a scent trail across the picked rows of corn. Using a bottle of Buck Stop's X-Cel in one hand and a bottle of Charge in the other, I squeezed out a few drops every other row. When I reached my waiting site, I put on my Scent-Lok liner and then the Shape Shifter suit. Once I was ready, I eased onto my wooden stool and settled in for the late-afternoon hunt.

THE SHADOW EMERGES

As darkness approached, the Shadow drew nearer, no longer a mysterious form. My eyes saw him plainly as a magnificent whitetail. He was a huge buck, both in antlers and body, and my heart raced.

I soon realized the buck was following my scent trail, stopping, sniffing the ground, and lip-curling as he slowly crossed the cut cornfield toward the decoy. It took him more than15 minutes to cover the distance, and I was nearly trembling by then.

The buck wasn't by himself, however. Standing in front of me was an old doe and her triplets. I had to account for their eyes as well as the buck's, but I managed to slowly stand without spooking any of them. The buck was now about 30 yards to my left, and I started counting points: 1-2-3-4-5. Oh my! What about the other side? 1-2-3-4-5-6.

"Oh, don't flub this up!" I told myself.

I snapped the release onto my bowstring and the buck stopped in his tracks. He had heard that little click, and now we stood like two stone warriors. We faced each other, waiting with determination for the other to move. Then one of the doe's triplets ran toward the buck. He looked toward the small doe, now less than 20 yards. Everything was happening too fast! The buck was now quartering slightly away. A few more steps and he would be out of range.

I came to full draw and my eyes focused on my bow's top sight pin. I put it behind his right shoulder. Without hesitation I pulled the trigger and watched my arrow disappear into his body. As the buck ran off, his front legs looked bowed and he struggled to keep his legs under him.

I was shaking and struggling to breathe as I almost toppled onto the wooden

This decoy is positioned where Judy's 11-pointer stood when she made her killing shot at less than 20 yards. Even though Judy didn't use a blind, the buck never knew she was nearby. Her outline can be seen in this photo, directly behind the buck's right flank.

stool. Seconds later I opened my backpack and dug for the cell phone to call Herman. After he said hello I babbled all kinds of details, hogging the conversation. He was soon on his way.

As I waited for him, I decided to get up and look for the buck. Darkness now enveloped the field and my flashlight batteries had little juice. I couldn't see any blood in the yellowing beam. Then I turned toward the woods and swept the flashlight's feeble beam along the field's edged. Somehow the weak light revealed the buck's white belly. I walked over, checked to make sure it was dead, and called Herman again to tell him the good news.

COMPANY ARRIVES

Meanwhile, coyotes found the blood trail and then they found me with the buck. I shone the small flashlight beam around and counted 10 large coyotes surrounding me and my buck. I patted the buck's massive antlers and told him I was leaving. Ten hungry coyotes were too many for me to handle.

I hadn't gotten far when I spotted the lights of Herman's Bronco bouncing across the field. When we met, I again babbled details until Herman made it clear he wanted to see the buck.

When we got back to the site, the coyotes were gone. Herman took one look at the buck and said we needed more help, so we made the necessary calls.

My cousin Jerry arrived on an ATV and Herman dug out 100 feet of ski rope from the Bronco. We backed the four-wheeler up against a big tree and loaded the 300-pound buck onto its front rack. Jerry's 300-pound frame on the four-wheeler's seat provided the counterbalance. Herman then tied the ATV to his Bronco, and we proceeded to haul the massive buck out of the woods and across the cornfield.

Jerry was in awe of the buck's tremendous antlers and body size. I asked him if this was the buck I had been hunting more than two years. He looked at me and nodded yes.

Herman smiled and said, "Well, that buck isn't just a shadow anymore."

The buck's undressed weight was a whopping 330 pounds, and his 11-point crown featured unbelievable mass that held its own far up the main beams. The antlers' green gross score was 172-7/8, and the buck's teeth indicated it was at least 6-1/2 years old.

I was especially proud of that buck. The only reason I got him was because I followed my instincts. I was confident that conventional setups like tree stands and ground blinds wouldn't work. I had stumbled across the Shape Shifter suit, and somehow I knew it was the only way I would ever arrow that buck.

CONCLUSION

Do Northern Cheyenne believe in shape shifting? You bet. That trophy buck looked right through me without recognizing the threat. Sure, I was also wearing a Scent-Lok liner, but my wool camo Shape Shifter suit made the biggest difference. I couldn't wait to bowhunt the shadows again. In fact, I silently warned the area's big bucks, "The Shape Shifter is now your shadow!" ■

22

AN ANCIENT QUEST FOR CARIBOU

I sat alone inside the small, dark room with log walls, listening to a drum beat grow louder and faster. Thickening smoke from a small fire at the room's center burned my eyes.

A tall, slender man walked from a corner of the room. He was a tribal elder, and he motioned for me to rise. He then placed an amulet around my neck—a 2,000-year-old piece of ivory with a caribou etched upon its shiny surface. The elders somehow knew one of my future destinations would include the caribou's land, but it was up to me to discover their reason for honoring me with the amulet.

The author poses with her last-minute bull caribou, taken in 2001 in northern Quebec. Judy overcame her fear of flying, as well as her fear of water, to reach this remote region, and was down to the final ten minutes of her bowhunt when the bull appeared.

Over the years, a few caribou outfitters had invited me to bowhunt with them, but my fear of water and flying prevented it. Then, almost six years after receiving the amulet, another caribou outfitter—Andre Threlfall—asked what it would take to get me to bowhunt caribou.

I told him I feared water, flying in general, and small planes specifically. The idea of flying hundreds of miles over tundra and large bodies of water scared me even more than tree stands. Confident that he would never agree to my conditions, I told Andre I would go only if he sat beside me the entire flight.

He then spoke a two-letter word that changed my life: "OK."

I was shocked into silence. Andre said he would leave his base camp, and fly with Herman and me to his lake camp and stay with us. My mind raced. As much as I feared such a trip, I had to stand by my words. I tried to act happy as Herman and Andre laid out the Quebec map and showed me the campsites and river setups.

I grasped the caribou-etched amulet in fear and held it tightly. Once again I wondered why the amulet meant so much to the elders and why they chose me as its bearer? I was the wrong Indian for this spirit quest. My Cheyenne ancestors had never seen a caribou. They lived on the Plains and hunted buffalo. But the amulet and its etching seemed to have almost mystical powers. My idle hands constantly reached for it and rubbed its smooth ivory surface. And as the intervening months flew by, my fears finally subsided, giving way to anticipation and excitement.

THE JOURNEY BEGINS

My fears returned suddenly a few days before our August 2001 trip, and they lingered during the long drive to Montreal. We barely slept that night in the motel.

We caught a morning flight to Schafferville, where we met up with Andre. That evening at his base camp, he reviewed his maps and caribou routes with us, and introduced us to his floatplane pilot, Jean Boisvert. Andre had warned the pilot of my fears, and Jean assured me that I need not worry.

Early the next morning we loaded the plane and they put me in the co-pilot seat. As Jean turned the floatplane around for its long take-off run down the lake, I noticed a huge stone cross near the lakeside, glistening in the new day's sunlight. I turned and asked Andre about the beautiful cross, but he apparently didn't hear me.

After leaving base camp and riding upstream in a cedar square-stern canoe, the Kovars arrived on a remote island for their first hunt. Herman and their guide went scouting for a setup, leaving Judy by the canoe to rest. But she soon spotted caribou nearby, and when this cow came within range, Judy arrowed the first caribou of her life.

As we flew above all that forest, tundra and water, Herman and Andre chatted and watched for caribou. I just sat nervously, watching Jean fly. Our landing on Lake Mussett was as soft and perfect as Jean had promised. Only then did Herman tell me

With their cedar canoe loaded with caribou meat and antlers, Judy and her guide head down the river back to base camp.

that the cross overlooking the base camp's lake was built after a floatplane crashed years ago, killing all aboard.

As I stepped onto the dock at Lake Mussett, the wildness of that country and terrain began to sink in. No lights, no people, just a few rough hunting cabins for shelter. All we heard was howling wolves each night. We watched the northern lights for entertainment.

The only way in and out of the vast wilderness was by floatplane. We were advised to remain wary and move carefully. A serious injury could mean a lingering death, and a foolish decision could deliver a sudden fatal blow. Mother Nature doesn't suffer fools and foolish behavior anywhere, but in caribou country there's simply no safety net.

We soon saw how dramatically conditions could change. The lake was nearly flat as glass when we landed, but before long it transformed into a monster, with five- to six-foot white-capped waves. The sky could be just as fearsome. On one frightening day, sheets of rain pelted us like hail stones, and the winds turned well-aimed arrows toward rocks that twisted those strong aluminum shafts into pretzels.

GET OUT THERE!

Even so, our guide, Jean wouldn't let us cower inside our cabin. Each day started with a 4:30 a.m. breakfast, and then we climbed into huge cedar canoes, following a river to destinations only a guide could ever find.

The first day, Herman, Jean and I planned to bowhunt an area known for its waterfalls and small islands. Caribou use the small islands while swimming across the river. Those river journeys required Herman and I to climb out and walk around rapids on three occasions while Jean walked the canoe through.

When we finally arrived, I needed to rest. Meanwhile, Jean and Herman went looking for a bowhunting setup. Suddenly, I noticed caribou swimming the river and heading for our little island. I was no longer tired!

I quickly set up where I could intercept them and waited for the right animal and the perfect shot. When the huge cow leading the group climbed the riverbank and shook off the water, I came to full draw. My top pin settled on her vitals and my finger touched the release. My first caribou was down moments later.

Jean congratulated me and started to quarter the meat and cape her out. When he finished those tasks, we looked for Herman, who had disappeared. Not to worry.

Judy never felt comfortable riding in the outfitters' sturdy cedar canoes, but she knew they were the only way she would ever reach caribou country. These workhorse canoes carry large, heavy loads without bogging down.

Herman had his own situation at the island's far end. He had arrowed a huge bull with double shovels and many feather points.

We returned to camp, where supper was waiting, and we relived the day's hunts and events. The night that followed kept us restless, as the winds howled and rain pelted the roof of our cabin. As morning arrived, the storm worsened and the winds turned the pretty lake into a maelstrom. All we could do that day was check equipment and watch the storm as Jean and Andre planned the next day's hunt. With luck, I would get my chance to arrow a caribou bull.

The weather had improved by the next morning, so we again piled into the cedar canoe and headed up the rapids toward the falls. My body ached as we again walked the shoreline and passed the third rapids. When we arrived, I struggled to get out of the canoe. Jean offered his hand and pointed to the rock where I should step. My tired, stiff leg refused to move.

Soon I had one leg on the rock and the other leg locked to the canoe! The canoe, of course, continued for the lake. Jean grasped at my coat but missed, then he grabbed for my hands, but he was too late for both. I fell into the icy lake and couldn't help but laugh at myself. Jean, however, saw no humor in the accident. He kept repeating, "Judy hurt? Why do you laugh?"

Jean and Herman helped me out of the lake, and my check for injuries revealed only a bruised ego. Jean made me stay in the canoe for the last rapids as he pulled and pushed through the swift water. Once we arrived at the island, the hours clicked by as we watched for caribou. At the end of the island, we saw a small bull walk to the shoreline, drink and walk back into dense pines.

SHORT ON TIME

Soon after, Jean checked his watch and said we only had about 10 minutes left to bowhunt before we had to head back. My hands searched for the caribou amulet and I looked up at the blue sky and her clouds. I wondered why I was here. What would the elders think of their "chosen one" now? I fear flying and I can't even swim, but here I was in northern Quebec, accessible only by air or boat, with much of the terrain still frozen in time from the Ice Age.

My cold left hand searched my coat pocket for the last pinch of the elder's blessed tobacco. After a silent prayer, I threw the offering into the air. As I bowed my head, my eyes caught movement. A bull was swimming toward the island! I reached for my bow and calculated where and which trail he would follow. I dropped to my knees and—half crawling, half duck waddling—reached the thick Labrador bush. With heart racing and hands trembling, I nocked an arrow.

The bull walked from the river, shook the water from his huge body, and then looked down the shoreline. If he stayed along the shore, I had no chance of cutting him off. I whispered silently, "I've given of myself. I've given all things a hunter must give of herself. Am I not worthy of this great animal? Give me the chance to arrow this bull. Let me decide its fate."

The bull turned and looked my way, and with his first step onto the shoreline I came to full draw. In a matter of moments only a few feet separated us. The bull looked at me. Its eyes showed no fear, and at less than six yard he bowed his velvet-covered antlered crown and turned broadside. I touched the release and the arrow's red- and white-barred feathers disappeared into the bull's chest.

No reaction! He just stood there. I pulled another arrow from the quiver and fumbled to nock it. I glanced at the bull and met his eyes again. As the bull walked away, I noticed my first arrow lying on the tundra.

I never took that second shot. I watched the bull walk a few feet and go down. He was mine now, and I admired him. His great velvet antlers were like no other animal I had bowhunted. Jean gave me a big hug and shook my hand while Herm took pictures. I had arrowed this great bull in the final minutes on the last day of our hunt.

Herm handed me my tobacco pouch, which should have been empty, but he had unrolled a few cigarettes and dumped their tobacco in the pouch. I gave an offering to the four winds and sprinkled some over the bull's body.

Jean expertly converted the bull into meat, quarters and hide, and then we were back in the canoe, returning to Camp Mussett as evening shadows began cloaking the river and lake.

Jean and his helper worked late, skinning capes and salting hides. I lay in my bunk and listened to the wolves, wind and rain. The next day our guides and cook were tearful as we left. The weather was changing quickly, so our floatplane landed without delay and Jean loaded up the meat boxes and equipment. We dispensed with our hugs, kisses and tears equally fast. The return flight was as smooth as the pilot could make it, but strong winds shoved the plane around so much that the sight of our base camp brought great relief!

With time winding down on her long-awaited caribou bowhunt, Judy arrowed this bull when it walked within six yards of her. The big bull didn't react when her arrow first sliced through its chest, but went down moments later.

REPORTING IN

Upon our return home, I called the elder and reported that my quest had produced two caribou. I had bowhunted the wilds of northern Quebec, traveled in canoes, and taken six airplane rides. The elders had shown me how to conquer my fears and reach my bowhunting potential.

When I stood before the elder once again, my hands offering the amulet back to him, he cupped his hands around mine and refused to accept it.

"You keep and wear it. Remember the ancient ones before you," he said. "When are you going back?" ■

23

WITHIN THE JAWS OF NA'HKOHE

Evening shadows slipped through shafts of light, bringing with them twilight's sounds and animals. My eyes scanned the darkening forest near Otter Lake in Quebec, searching for that special "spirit" bear.

When a bear suddenly appeared from the gloom, I nudged my guide's shoulder. Bob and I looked at the bear, a small sow, and declined to take a shot. Soon after, a huge, thinly furred raccoon appeared on the path paralleling our blind. We didn't give it much attention until it got near the sow, whose head was buried inside the barrel. When the sow pulled out and spotted the raccoon, she gave four deep woofs and ran toward our blind!

After those first couple of woofs, I grabbed Bob's right arm. The sow was inches away when she decided to climb a small, dead tree, but that little tree was connected to the front of my blind! I looked at Bob, hoping my experienced guide had a solution. Minutes passed and then the sow clambered down and raced into the forest. As I slowly regained my composure, I felt Bob prying my clenched fingers from his arm.

I looked at him through the bug netting and whispered, "Sorry about that," and smiled in embarrassment.

That incident made me the target of many jokes and much ridicule the next few days, but that was easier to endure than the tattoos that my grip had burned into Bob's arm. Those black-and-blue bruises showed the outline of my fingers for days.

MY BROTHER THE BEAR

The Northern Cheyenne people have a special kinship with the black bear, and we tell many stories about this particular species, which we call "Na'hkoke" and sometimes refer to as our brother. Indians consider Na'hkoke nearly mystical because it possesses great strength and can walk on its hind legs.

Therefore, when Herman and I arrived at Claude Marchand's bear camp on Otter Lake, I asked Bob, "How is the bear's hiding place?"

He answered, "The bear's hiding place is fine and he waits for his Indian sister. Tomorrow we will travel to bear's special place and build your blind."

The phrase "bear's hiding place" refers to a story told to Art Young and Saxton Pope by Ishi, the last Yahi Indian from California.

Just as Ishi described his "special" hunting spot, I too arrowed and put to sleep Na'hkohe in a place now hallowed.

AN EMOTIONAL PLACE

I felt unusually emotional when my feet again touched that familiar ground a year later. I walked to the bait barrel, looked over my left shoulder, and was surprised by what I saw. There, still woven together, were the dry, brown-needled pine boughs and small trees that formed last year's ground blind. I whispered the distance as I stepped off the yardage to the granite boulder that would again protect my back.

Judy Kovar poses with her "Na'hkoke," the Northern Cheyenne name for black bears. She shot the bruin in Quebec in spring 2003. The Cheyenne consider Na'hkoke nearly mystical because of its great strength and ability to walk on its hind legs.

I then turned to face the bait barrel and Herman. He asked, "Is it still less than eight yards from the barrel to your feet?"

I nodded yes. He shook his head in disapproval and walked away, mumbling something about being married to a crazy woman with a death wish.

Herman had been worrying aloud for weeks, deeply concerned about my bear tactics. I was surprised by his tone. Never before had he voiced concern for my bowhunting decisions. Worse, our daily skirmishes had become obvious to all.

When I looked at the ground inside my new blind, I saw three piles of bear scat! I hoped Herman wouldn't come close enough to see them. He didn't like me bowhunting bears from the ground.

I turned my attention to the ground inside my new blind so my eyes wouldn't meet Herman's. Inside were three piles of bear scat! I hoped Herman wouldn't come close enough to see them. I looked around outside the blind and immediately spotted four more piles of scat, and saw that Herman had found four others. I dreaded our return to camp, because I sensed Herman and I would again discuss my options!

Standing behind the blind's walls, I checked and rechecked my shooting lanes.

Meanwhile, Bob filled the barrel with two 80-pound boxes of sweets, and then walked over, entered the blind and set up his stool. I was confused and then awe-struck. I had expected to be left alone. I whispered, "Bob, are you going to sit with me?" He assured me that was his plan.

Earlier, Claude had advised us to not visit the blind for four days except to place bait each morning.

When the time arrived to sit there to hunt, tall afternoon shadows engulfed most of the blind. I watched Bob dump another 80-pound box of sweets into the barrel, and place a container of Buck Stop's Bear Bait atop an oak stump.

I was already excited. My shaking hand reached for an arrow and I clicked its nock onto my bow-string. Bob entered the blind and settled in behind the fragile pine boughs, resting a 12-gauge shotgun on his lap. I hadn't yet sat down, so I turned to check the granite boulder, which was veiled by shadows. As I glanced behind me, something caught my eye: a feather … actually, two feathers, both resting between the green ferns. One was from an owl and the other from a raven. I touched Bob's shoulder and asked why he had put them there.

Most folks know nothing about such matters, but many Native Americans are obsessed with feathers. In our cultures, feathers foretell or honor special places, ceremonies or achievements. Bob looked at the feathers and assured me that neither he nor any other guide had put them there.

THE HUNT UNFOLDS

During the next few days, Bob and I saw several bears and our repeat customer, the small sow. Plus, we learned our eight-yard shooting distance didn't allow us to twitch when bears were nearby. Simply shifting our weight on the stools sometimes panicked a visiting bear. I was also certain the bears could hear me breathing.

I decided we must change tactics. It was time to try my Shape-Shifter suit from Sleeping Indian. As you might recall from a previous chapter, that suit helped me arrow a monster whitetail the year before. Would it work on bears?

I was already wearing my Scent-Lok suit, so all I had to do was slip into the Shape-Shifter. Besides, it offered other benefits. When Herman and others questioned my ground-hunting tactics, I jokingly reminded them that I wear extra-large camo so hungry bears can bite only the large folds in my clothing, not flesh and bone!

The next day, we set up in a ground blind 20 yards from our bait. I wondered to myself if today would be the day. Bob settled onto his stool while I slipped into the Shape-Shifter suit. As the afternoon shadows surrendered to darkness, the unusually calm air gave way to a stiff breeze and threatening clouds. When I returned my attention to the barrel, my eyes locked onto a bear. Behind that bear was another bear.

My heart quickened and my mouth turned to dry cotton. Once again, my hand reached for Bob, but he already knew from my body language that a bear was near. As we focused on the two bruins, a loud roar nearby startled us. A third bruin was present, but it never came to the barrel. We could hear it swatting and sometimes

The author bowhunts bears the same way she hunts deer: from the ground. As with her deer hunts, Judy relied on the Shape-Shifter suit to keep her hidden when the black bear came to the bait site.

breaking brush and small trees, and also ripping at grass and dirt. In other words, this bear was acting aggressive, and twice bluff-charged our blind. Bob assured me the bear was all bluster, but if those false charges were meant to frighten me, they were working!

The bear was acting aggressive, and twice bluff-charged our blind. Bob assured me the bear was all bluster, but if those false charges were meant to frighten me, they were working!

Our attention again turned to the two bears near the barrel. I was waiting for one of them to start eating, but they wouldn't allow each other the privilege. They were growling at each other. Then they started trading swats. Next, they broke into a full-fledged fight!

As the battle raged, the third bear joined the fray. Fur was literally flying inches from our blind. Bob and I weren't so sure we liked our front-row seats to this match-up! When they paused, the largest bear kept pushing and breaking brush while the second bear stayed head-to-head with his foe.

DON'T MIND US!

When the threesome squared off again, the middle bear kept his muzzle facing his opponent but steadily backed up. Then, before we knew it, the two bears were inside our blind, wildly biting and swatting each other! They had no idea they were fighting between two humans as Bob and I crashed sideways from our stools. All I could see was fur, claws and teeth. I tried getting back up, but the battling bruins knocked me down again. This time I toppled between the boulder and my stool, and then watched in terror as a bear bit a chunk of the foam cushion from my stool.

I jerked my leg away, but the bear reacted instantly and bit a mouthful of wool strips from my Shape-Shifter suit. I kicked what was left of my stool at the brawling bears. One of them took one swipe with a front paw and smacked the stool across the remains of our blind. About then, Bob scrambled to his feet and yelled at the combatants. Finally, they realized they weren't alone and ran in opposite directions.

I toppled between the boulder and my stool, and then watched in terror as a bear bit a chunk of the foam cushion from my stool. I jerked my leg away, but the bear reacted instantly and bit a mouthful of wool strips from my Shape-Shifter suit.

Our blind now looked like a war zone. We inventoried our body parts and checked for injuries. As my adrenaline dropped, I started shaking. I unzipped my Shape-Shifter suit, expecting to find blood soaking my clothes, but was shocked to find no leaks! And when I lifted the leg the bear had bitten, I noticed only a couple of welts from its canine teeth. Somehow, neither of us had been injured, but we were badly shaken!

"Let's let everything settle down after all that ruckus," Bob said. Once we returned to normal, we headed back to camp. I had no doubt the Shape-Shifter suit had saved my leg and knee from Na'hkohe's jaws.

After we reached camp and told our story, I couldn't wait to climb into our tent and sleep. I felt exhausted—mentally and physically drained. I thought sleep would come quickly, but every time I closed my eyes I saw the bear's jaws clenching my leg. Almost as bad, I knew Herman now had more ammo to use against me! We didn't talk about it. His looks said it all.

BACK TO THE BLIND

The temperatures were rising when Bob and I crawled back into the blind the next day. My Shape-Shifter suit soon became hot and uncomfortable, and the black-fly hordes and huge mosquitoes became nonstop nuisances. Dark clouds covered the horizon, signaling that we would lose daylight early.

As dusk approached, a dark figure silently appeared and lumbered to the bait barrel, which was lying on its side. With one quick move, the bear picked up the barrel and set it down vertically. I nodded to Bob that this was the bear I wanted. I stood slowly, my bow and arrow up and ready. When the bear grabbed a chunk of sweet bait and walked about 30 yards without offering a shot, I started to sit down. Bob wouldn't allow it. He whispered, "No! It's coming back. Stay put."

Sure enough, the bruin soon stood before us once more and our eyes met. I silently whispered an Indian prayer that told the bear I was there to take its life. My prayer promised I would honor it before and after death, because I, too, am a predator.

Earlier, I had honored the bear with a tobacco and sweet-grass ceremony. My prayer said I stood on sacred ground and knew the black bear is the Northern Cheyenne's brother.

I shifted to the left and covered the bear's vitals with my brightly colored pin. I touched the release's trigger and watched the red- and white-barred feathers shoot into the bear.

Bob again asked if I had a clear shot. "No," I whispered. I then stepped to my right and looked again. Before me stood two dead pine trees about three inches in diameter and about eight to 10 inches apart. Could I make the shot?

I shifted to the left and covered the bear's vitals with my brightly colored pin. I had only seconds for this window to work. I touched the release's trigger and watched the red- and white-barred feathers shoot into the bear. The bear's roar thundered through the darkening forest, and it disappeared into the thick pine boughs and deadfalls.

This time it was Bob grabbing my shoulder. He asked excitedly, "What the heck was that?"

I stared at him and replied, "What the heck was what?"

He asked if I had seen the fire that came from the bear's back.

"I saw sparks and fire come out of that bear," he said. "You didn't see it, Judy?"

I had not. We got out of the blind and hunted for my arrow, but darkness now covered everything. Our search for my bear, however, didn't take long, and we soon had it loaded for our return to camp.

A SUCCESSFUL NIGHT

A tarp partially hid the bear in the back of our vehicle, so Herman didn't notice it as he walked over and laid his bow and fanny pack inside. Bob cautioned him to be quiet so as not to wake our guest. Herman looked at me, then Bob, and asked, "You guys arrowed a bear?"

Bob then told Herman about the fire bursting from my bear's back. As we talked about the bruin, I looked up at the heavens and saw the northern lights dancing overhead. I watched those lights all the way back to Otter Lake, fascinated by the infinite variety of their gleaming undulations.

After arriving in camp, we learned that four others had tagged bruins that evening. Claude walked over to our vehicle and hugged me.

"Claude, did you see the northern lights?" I asked.

"Yes, it's a sign from your Grandfather Wolf. Your grandfather is very proud of his Indian, just as I am. Many hunters would have quit and gone home after what happened to you. You're one heck of a bowhunter, Indian!"

Late that evening, I walked alone to the sleeping bruin and honored him once more, talking to him softly and offering tobacco to the four directions. I then emptied the remaining tobacco onto his chest.

Late that evening, I walked alone to the sleeping bruin and honored him once more, talking to him softly and offering tobacco to the four directions. I then emptied the remaining tobacco onto his chest. I looked skyward, lighted a braid of sweet-grass, and finished my prayers.

Then Herman walked out of the shadows, his arms outstretched. He congratulated me with a hug and tried to explain his concerns. With tears in our eyes, we returned to our cabin.

EXPLAINING THE FIRE

The next morning after the photo sessions, Bob returned from my sacred hunting site and handed me my arrow shaft, which was now minus its broadhead. He told me he had figured out the source of the sparks and flames from my shot. He had positioned a granite boulder to keep the bait barrel level, and my broadhead smashed into the rock after passing through my bear. Bob said the boulder bore large impact scars, as well as an etched trail angling into the sky. Bob said again it had been an awesome sight. I was sorry I missed it.

Since that hunt, some folks have again suggested I change my bowhunting tactics or start hunting from tree stands. They should save their breath. It won't happen. I feel safer going eye to eye with bears than I do sitting high above ground on a small platform. Besides, those bears never knew we were there when they tumbled into our blind. It was mere coincidence they ended up there while fighting.

I respect my brother the black bear and I honor him whenever appropriate. Do I fear Na'hkoke? Only when he holds my leg within his jaws! ■

24

THE BOWHUNTING SPIRIT

She summer and autumn of 2005 brought extremely dry and hot conditions, which plagued the opening of Illinois' archery season . . . along with high humidity, starving flies and hateful mosquitoes.

That early archery season was torturous, with temperature hitting the 90s. In my search for relief, I wore Scent-Lok's BaseSlayer undergarments and covered them with the Savanna series clothing to make the mosquitoes' smorgasbord less accessible. But no matter what I tried, I sweated profusely. And don't tell me that men sweat and women perspire! Oppressive heat and humidity don't care whether you're male or female. They make everyone sweat equally.

The author poses with her ninth Pope & Young buck, which she arrowed in October 2005 while bowhunting from a farm shed overlooking a field. After placing scent and staking down her decoy, Judy settled in to wait. When the buck appeared, she let it get within 20 yards before releasing her arrow.

Suddenly, bowhunting brought nothing by misery. It was impossible to make a stalk or sit in a blind. The constant buzzing of insects drove me crazy, ruining every stalk. Even with its top unzipped, my favorite ground blind was too hot and way too inviting for my bloodthirsty enemies! I had to quickly find a solution because I couldn't focus on whitetails.

Finally, I stood on the edge of our clover and turnip patch, and scanned the farm. Before me stood an old horse barn made of rough-sawn oak, and adjoining it was a corn crib. That old barn was the first building my parents built after buying the farm. They had cut down many oak trees with a crosscut saw, and then used their horse team to pull the huge logs to the sawmill to be cut into lumber. They'd used that lumber to build the farmhouse, barns, cribs, chicken house and deep-well ice-house.

After looking around, I walked slowly to what had been the horses' living quarters. As I peered inside, I saw many of the old reins, doubletrees, horseshoes and other equipment. Once inside the barn, I discovered I could watch three of the farm's fields from one location. The open windows offered a breeze, and the room provided plenty of space to hide my movements when the insects arrived.

Once inside the barn, I discovered I could watch three of the farm's fields. The windows offered a breeze, and the room provided space to hide my movements when insects arrived.

MOVE-IN DAY

The next morning I moved in and checked the windows and shooting lanes. The only problem was my chair. It was too low to allow me to look easily through the windows and watch for whitetails. When I returned home and walked downstairs to share my findings with Herman, I found him sitting on an old barstool, cresting some arrows. The stool was tall and it swiveled. Say goodbye to your barstool, Herman!

I returned to the barn the next day, carrying my new hunting seat. After verifying that the barstool would serve my needs, I went outside to check and reposition my scouting cameras, and then I checked and doctored two of my mock scrapes. One scrape beneath a walnut tree grabbed my attention because it was turning into a large, dominant scrape.

That afternoon I grabbed my bow and settled in atop the barstool so I could watch the small clover and turnip field. A couple of hours later, a parade of whitetails entered the field. First came some mature does, followed by yearlings and fawns. Before long, 13 whitetails stood before me, but none were bucks. Still, I was overjoyed. When the day's bowhunt ended, I was determined to challenge or enrage any dominant buck roaming the Kovar farm!

After gathering the film and "smart cards" from my scouting cameras, I drove into town to get them developed. Later, my first hint that the film contained a special whitetail came when I returned to the film counter and saw about seven employees pointing at the pictures and talking excitedly.

To my astonishment, the photos showed nine monster bucks! Three were nontypicals, six were typicals, and all were Pope & Young candidates with estimated scores from the 130s to 170s.

Some pictures showed several bucks in the field at the same time, and all of them were in the same small hillside patch of clover and turnips. It seemed that small food plot was the place to be every afternoon and evening.

My mind was now in overdrive, crafting a new plan. I have long relied on deer decoys to catch the eye and attention of feeding whitetails or to challenge any would-be rivals. More recently, I had started using an almost full-motion decoy, the MoJo, which I can remotely control from my blind.

Before dawn on October 27, I returned to the old horse barn, brimming with excitement and anticipation. After setting up my decoy, I went to the scrape to apply my scents and deer potions.

When the decoy first arrived, I had studied its posture and internal parts, and decided I could make it even more lifelike. The MoJo has a grooved coat to resemble whitetail hair, but it's basically one color. So I decided to make it more visible with color and depth. For every hair groove, I applied a stroke of black permanent marker, and for every three black marks I followed with a stroke of brown and then a dark gray. The job took almost four days and more than 14 permanent markers, but the result was magnificent. After it dried thoroughly, I sprayed the decoy with an unscented odor-eliminating spray.

BACK TO THE BARN

As our season slipped into late October, I was now ready for a showdown with a monster whitetail. On the morning of October 27, I returned to my spot in the old horse barn, brimming with excitement and anticipation. After setting up my decoy, I visited the nearby scrape to apply my scents and deer potions. The scrape now covered a six-foot square and held hundreds of tracks. Next I added a few drops of buck semen to the scrape. I hadn't tried this before, but I had heard it was producing good results for other bowhunters.

I then walked inside the barn to begin my wait upon the barstool. Sometime after dawn, I heard leaves rustling, and then a button buck entered the small food plot. Next, the mature does and their fawns appeared and started feeding. None of them seemed to notice the decoy, so I grabbed its remote control and pressed the button. Two of the fawns started running and playing as they moved toward my fake deer. The old does watched but continued feeding. One of the fawns ran behind the decoy and tried to nuzzle it.

Then the fawn suddenly bolted, and every other whitetail fled. What was happening? Soon I heard breaking limbs and grunts coming from the woods below the decoy. As quickly as the whitetails had disappeared, they reappeared. Once again I had nearly 20 does, fawns and yearlings in sight, but I could still hear leaves and brush popping inside the woods.

Then I saw him. A buck faced my position and the decoy, but it was still hugging the early-morning shadows. His nose tested the wind and his eyes locked on two of the older does, which were still accompanied by their fawns. When the wind picked up and swirled, the buck's head snapped immediately toward the scrape. He lip-curled and stepped out of the shadows.

Then I saw him. A buck faced my position and the decoy, but it was still hugging the early-morning shadows. His nose tested the wind and his eyes locked on two of the older does.

I whispered to myself, as if Grey Wolf were beside me, "Get off the rack! Get it together! Watch his nose and body language."

The 10-pointer lowered his head and ran after one of the older does, but when the wind swirled the buck again reacted to the mock scrape. With his head down, he headed for the scrape and boldly entered it. His antlers worked the dirt and overhanging branches, and then he stepped back a few feet from the walnut tree. I wasn't prepared for his next move: The buck suddenly leaped, hitting the tree so hard that his rear quarters left the ground!

He then backed up and stared at my decoy, his ears laid back. He walked sideways toward it, grunting deeply. If he continued on this path he would pass less than 20 yards from me. I locked my release onto the string and with one strong pull I anchored. The buck again lowered his head and rack, setting himself up for a battle.

SUCCESS! OR NOT?

When I released my arrow, the buck spun around, searching to see what had stung him, but he didn't run. He just stood and stared as the field emptied. He then walked to the woods' edge and stood still, swayed slightly, and lowered his head.

Then I heard a noise I had never before heard from a whitetail: a bawl, much like a bear's death bawl. But still he didn't fall. In fact, he stood there when I slipped out of the barn, retreated from the food plot and called Herman. When he arrived, he followed me back to the food plot as I relived the morning's events.

We entered the food plot; the buck was no longer there! But surely he couldn't have gone far, we thought. We found the blood trail, and as we followed it, we noticed the leaves and dirt were torn up. Just before we started downhill into a steep, rocky ravine, Herman said, "I sure hope that buck didn't roll all the way to the creek bed."

My heart began to break as we moved several feet without any blood sign. Herman was slightly ahead of me, and I heard him say, "Judy, come to me."

When he stepped aside, I could see my buck piled up against a small elm, its back legs wrapped around its trunk. That little tree had kept the buck from falling 10 to 12 feet down the ravine. Herman and I looked at each other and sat down. How could we get the buck out of this mess?

How? With time and lots of work! It took us nearly four hours, 200 feet of nylon rope, strategically placed brush and dead trees, and our four-wheel-drive ATV to extract the buck from that ravine. The retrieval was worth the effort, of course. The buck scores 136-0/8 on the Pope & Young scoring system.

Once we had the buck "topside" and loaded up, we passed the wooden door of the horse barn. I gave it a glance and smiled. Looking skyward, I whispered thanks to Mother and Grey Wolf for all their help.

Herman might never get his barstool back. At least not during autumn!! ■

25

REFORMING A CIRCLE FROM ITS ASHES

Many years have passed since my parents died. Being an only child, I had the heart-tugging tasks of cleaning up and maintaining our old home, its acreage and the orchards in the time since.

Eventually, snakes of every species and color claimed the old house as their home. Mice, rats and lizards scurried across the roof's shingles, constantly playing life-and-death games with the snakes below.

Yes, Mother Nature reclaimed the home place, and she encouraged every thorn, brier, thistle and weed to grow there, too. Elsewhere, wild grape vines and bittersweet laced their way around every tree in the orchard. The fruit trees clung to life, but most became scarred from peach-tree borers and other insects and disease.

Every time I bowhunted the farm during autumn 2004, my eyes reminded me of a hard truth my heart denied or ignored. Finally, I gave in. I knew what had to be done. With an unsteady hand and a tear sliding down my cheek, I lifted the phone and dialed up a bulldozer. Jim Davenport and I met at an agreed-upon time to assess the job, and then he gave me his estimate.

A few hours later his bulldozer was pushing out the once-beautiful plum, apple and cherry trees. Jim saw me watching, and stopped the bulldozer to ask if I approved of his work.

"Yeah," I answered. It was all I could say.

With the fruit trees pushed into a pile, Jim turned the bulldozer to my childhood home and started pushing on its east side. Even after a few well-placed assaults from the bulldozer, the house failed to crumble. Jim repositioned his machine and attacked from another direction. Again, even with the bulldozer pushing concrete sidewalks atop the house's hand-cut oak logs and boards, the structure failed to bow.

I sat in the fresh dirt and watched in amazement. That powerful bulldozer, with grey smoke billowing from its stack, was no small machine, yet it was being stymied by that old house!

The bulldozer next attacked from the remaining sides, and yet the house still stood! Jim tried to drive through it, but the oak logs anchoring the structure and supporting the roof proved stubborn. I sat in the freshly exposed dirt and watched in amazement. That powerful bulldozer, with grey smoke billowing from its stack, was being stymied by that old house!

When the time came to help nature reclaim the farm where she was raised, the author knew she had to be alone while supervising the demolition work. Judy and Herman Kovar traveled together through much of North America during the first 15 years of their marriage, but Herman understood Judy's need for solitude that mournful day.

GIVING BACK THE LAND

Tears welled in my eyes as I continued watching. I questioned my reasoning for this cleanup. I thought of all that work, all that determination my parents funneled into the house, and how they had built it from scratch. At the time, the only other manmade structure on their 160 acres was a small hand-laid limestone basement.

Even so, I knew this had to be done. Native Americans believe in returning the land to what it was before they built upon it.

My hand reached inside my jeans and retrieved a small package of elder-blessed tobacco. I mumbled a short prayer and tossed the tobacco to the east, west, north and south. I asked the "spirits" to understand why I was doing the cleanup, and to guide me through this closure. I stood alone on my family's ground, asking the spirits to allow this "circle of a new beginning" to resprout and grow.

My legs felt weak and I trembled. Just then, I heard a loud crack. When I opened my eyes, I saw the roof and three walls finally collapse. The roof and its oak timbers lay intact atop the walls momentarily, but Jim had no trouble crushing those remains with his bulldozer.

The house was now a pile of rubble, and my next heart-tugging task began. Jim moved his bulldozer away from the wood-pile that had once been my home, went to his truck and pulled out a tank of diesel fuel. He announced that he needed to head into town for a few hours because his machine had blown an oil line.

After he left, I felt inside a pocket for some matches. Then I picked up the diesel-fuel container and, with matches in hand, made the longest walk of my life to my home's crumpled remains.

Within minutes the old house's timbers were aflame. What had taken years to build, maintain and keep in my name was gone in little more than four hours.

I said another prayer, offered more tobacco to the four directions, and splashed fuel on the roof and one wall. Then I struck a match. Within minutes the old house's timbers were aflame. What had taken years to build, maintain and keep in my name was burned and gone in little more than four hours.

I can't explain the deep loneliness or sadness that followed. My childhood memories and my parents' dreams had turned to smoke and floated away. Then I looked at the maple tree in front and saw it still held the same dog-chain swing I had played on so many times as a girl.

My mother had planted that maple when they first acquired the farm from the bank. Father had tied the horse team too close to the sapling, and one of the horses had nipped off the top, causing it to grow four trunks instead of one.

TIME TO GO

Finally, evening shadows gently settled over the house's glowing embers, telling me I needed to go home to Herman. He had allowed me to handle this chore on my own. There was no pressure, just understanding. I needed time to deal with this painful task, and I needed to do it alone.

As I looked one last time at the smoking embers, all that stood was the flue from our wood furnace. It looked like a carved stone warrior, standing brave against all challengers. But I knew tomorrow it would be pushed into the basement with whatever the fire hadn't consumed. It wouldn't win the confrontation with Jim's bulldozer.

Grandfather! Grandfather! Have I made you proud?

Grandfather, I find comfort upon this land and in its animals. May my feet feel Mother Earth, and might she remember the skinny, raven-haired little Indian girl who started here.

I had come full circle and returned all that once was to its beginnings. The animals can again walk these lands north to south, east to west. And I will remember when the power of a machine, at least for a while, was no match for the spirits.

Grandfather, I find comfort upon this land and in its animals. May my feet feel Mother Earth, and might she remember the skinny, raven-haired little Indian girl who started here. ■

SAVE OUR HERITAGE

"Your Investment in the Future of Archery and Bowhunting"

The Save Our Heritage initiative comes from the Archery Trade Association and the Bowhunting Preservation Alliance. With the purchase of this book you are supporting programs that help grow the sports you love–archery and bowhunting. SOH book proceeds support community archery programs and parks; archery range building and refurbishing; in-school and after-school archery and bowhunting programs; and many more nationwide efforts to grow archery and protect and promote bowhunting.

Did You Know?

■ ATA has given grants totaling nearly $600,000 to help fund school-archery programs in nearly 40 states.

■ ATA is working to develop Community Archery Programs (CAPs) in urban/suburban areas in Alabama, Arizona, California, Illinois, Iowa, Michigan, Minnesota, Ohio, Tennessee and Nevada.

■ ATA partners with state wildlife agencies to fund archery or shooting program coordinators who lead CAP efforts on a local level.

■ ATA paid for a research study that analyzed the effectiveness of school archery programs and created the Insight brochure summarizing the results. The brochure helps administrators and others understand the value of school archery programs.

■ ATA created the Insight brochure, Archery, the Safe Sport, which is an invaluable tool when discussing the safety aspects of archery with school and recreation program administrators.

■ ATA education staff members created Explore Bowhunting, an introductory bowhunting curriculum available to educators and program managers.

■ ATA works with state agencies to locate archery parks in areas where kids, families and other community citizens recreate.

■ ATA works with state agencies to develop urban deer hunting opportunities.

■ ATA partnered with the U.S. Fish and Wildlife Service to offer more bowhunting opportunities on National Wildlife Refuges.

■ ATA has provided legal defense for private landowners whose right to bowhunt has been challenged by neighbors, local groups or even residential associations.

Your support of the Save Our Heritage program provides funds for these programs . . . and more.

WOODS N' WATER PRESS

Other titles available from the Save Our Heritage book program include:

208 pages, 140+ photos, color insert, Hardcover $24.95

208 pages, 80+ photos, color insert, Hardcover $24.95

208 pages, 100+ photos, color insert, Hardcover $24.95

240 pages, 80+ photos, color insert, Hardcover $24.95

240 pages, 100+ photos, Hardcover $24.95

208 pages, 80+ photos, color insert, Hardcover $24.95

176 pages, 70+ photos, Paperback $19.95

176 pages, 100+ photos, & DVD Paperback $24.95

176 pages, 140+ photos, color insert, Paperback $22.95

These are the ONLY books you can buy where a portion of every sale goes back to save your bowhunting heritage!

Ask for these exciting and informative titles at your local sporting goods dealer or order on-line at www.atabooks.com.
Call our office at 1-607-548-4011 or write to us at Woods N' Water Press, P.O. Box 10, South New Berlin, NY 13843 for a catalog.
We thank you for your support!